D1126327

THE
INTERNATIO
BUSINESSWON

THE
INTERNATIONAL
BUSINESSWOMAN

A Guide to Success
in the Global Marketplace

Marlene L. Rossman

BOWLING GREEN STATE UNIVERSITY
DISCARDED
BOWLING GREEN
STATE UNIVERSITY
LIBRARY
LIBRARIES

PRAEGER SPECIAL STUDIES • PRAEGER SCIENTIFIC

New York   •   Westport, Connecticut   •   London

Library of Congress Cataloging-in-Publication Data

Rossman, Marlene L.
    The international businesswoman.

    Bibliography: p.
    1. Women in business — Handbooks, manuals, etc.
    2. Negotiation in business — Handbooks, manuals, etc.
    I. Title.
    HD6054.3.R67   1986   650.1′024042   86-8156
    ISBN 0-275-92000-3 (alk. paper)
    ISBN 0-275-92001-1 (pbk. : alk. paper)

Copyright © 1986 by Praeger Publishers

All rights reserved. No portion of this book may be
reproduced, by any process or technique, without the
express written consent of the publisher.

Library of Congress Catalog Card Number: 86-8156
ISBN 0-275-92000-3 (alk. paper)
ISBN 0-275-92001-1 (pbk. : alk. paper)

First published in 1986

Praeger Publishers, 521 Fifth Avenue, New York, NY 10175
A division of Greenwood Press, Inc.

Printed in the United States of America

The paper used in this book complies with the Permanent
Paper Standard issued by the National Information Standards
Organization (Z39.48-1984).

10 9 8 7 6 5 4 3 2 1

Preface

I wrote *Women in International Business* for professional and university women who are intrigued and excited by the world of international business and want to learn more about opportunities open to them.

In 1984, I was asked to speak about my career to the Women's Career Forum at New York University's Graduate School of Business. The women overwhelmed me with questions about how they could prepare for a career in international business. I found that although there are a number of books about doing business overseas, none are unique to women entering this field. These women were asking the same questions that I had faced when I first entered this once all male preserve.

As I did research for this book, I listed the qualities that make for a successful international negotiator. I realized that the flexibility, patience and tolerance that characterize so many women are precisely the qualities so desperately needed in the international arena.

You don't have to travel overseas to use this book. International business is being conducted every day here in the United States. Wherever you are, if you have the skill, knowledge and determination, you'll find a world of opportunity waiting for you!

I'd like to thank a few people whose assistance and encouragement helped me write this book: the staff of Praeger Publishers, especially my editor, Alison Podel; Felicia Morales, who not only struggled to type the manuscript from my illegible handwriting, but offered many helpful suggestions; and my husband Elliot Silverman, without whom there wouldn't have been a book.

Contents

Contents

Introduction

The world is shrinking in every sense. Not only in communications and transportation (consider the Concorde, satellite and data networks) but commercially as well. "Global" advertising, marketing, planning, trading, manufacturing and joint venturing are not just buzzwords, but operating realities.

Since so much business is international in scope, we have learned that the only way to do volume business in the international market is to get out of the U.S. headquarters office and get on the road.

While many women are traveling within the United States and gaining acceptance as a result of their drive, competence and perseverance, the same thing is beginning to happen in the international arena.

In 1983, over 4 million Americans traveled overseas for business. A large group of Americans are also working for multinational corporations or are on long-term assignment for their company. In the past few years, women have begun to enter the international market in more than just token numbers.

The growth in international trade and travel is only one side of the story, however. There are still deep-seated cultural differences between the United States and other countries. A business traveler to Chicago, Riyadh, Buenos Aires or Milan may see the same Coca-Cola or Toyota signs in the airport in each city, but she will be mistaken if she thinks the business culture in each of the cities will be alike.

While negotiating sales and contracts in the United States is not an easy task, it is a good deal more difficult in the international marketplace. Misinterpreted signals, missed cues, overt errors, small slights and a host of unknowns can foul a deal. Not only can millions of dollars be lost, but future opportunities can be lost in a market forever. If a deal is lost because a businesswoman doesn't know the cultural norms, you can be sure that her company will never get another chance. Foreign executives are often a tightly knit social group, bound together by strong interpersonal relationships. A businesswoman who unknowingly breaks a social taboo may find other doors in that locale permanently closed.

On the other hand, a businesswoman who takes the time to become attuned to cultural considerations can negotiate contracts, make sales and, more importantly, open entire markets for her company.

The key to doing business overseas is to be well-prepared. First, you must arm yourself with extensive "hard skills," develop a confident personality and gain expertise in the product or service you are selling. Second, speaking the language of the country in which you are working is a great advantage. Even a few words make a difference. Political sophistication and knowing what *not* to say are often even more important than knowing what to say. Third, and most important, is learning the business culture. While business practices are different throughout the world, in most places overseas you must spend long hours getting to know your customer. In Latin America, the Middle East and the Orient especially, be prepared to have a few getting-acquainted meetings before getting down to business. You may feel you're drinking enough coffee or tea to float home on, but that's the way business is done. In those areas of the world, a relationship of trust must be established or your proposals will not be taken seriously.

What about doing business in countries not known for their liberal attitudes toward women? There are still some unspoken barriers to entry, but for the most part, a U.S. businesswoman, properly prepared, can succeed anywhere. While Western Europe and Latin America are somewhat more open to women, the businesswoman in many countries often is perceived as a "U.S. businessperson." You must do whatever you can to foster that image. A firm handshake and knowing how to present yourself go far to break down resistance. Always keep your sense of humor and think of how long it took the United States to accept women executives. As a woman, you probably couldn't have held your current position 20 years ago in the United States, so be patient with men in parts of the world that have rarely or never done business with a woman.

What about nonbusiness hours? The same rules apply as when doing business domestically. Try, if possible, to keep your business acquaintances just that. Romance and business do not mix very well anywhere in the world. That doesn't mean you must sit in your hotel room during your entire stay. There are many ways to meet interesting people overseas without mixing fun with work. Good bets are religious, trade and university affiliations where you can notify members in advance of your arrival. There is nothing like being welcomed into a home or club in a place 7,500 miles from home!

Increasingly, women are being presented with opportunities for business travel, long-term assignment or relocation overseas. While overseas long-term assignments used to be a place to dump managers or derail them from the fast track, nowadays quite the opposite is true. Long- and short-term overseas experience gives you a tremendous edge when back in the United States. While the world may be shrinking, your professional horizons will be expanding.

THE
INTERNATIONAL
BUSINESSWOMAN

1

Women in Business: A World of Opportunity

In this shrinking world, business is becoming global in scope, and new opportunities are appearing in many industries. In the past, women were often excluded from most significant business opportunities. There are those who argue that we still are. Last year, women on average earned less than 66 cents for each dollar paid to men. Battles are raging in the courts over "comparable worth," the argument that fields traditionally dominated by women should be paid equally to occupations traditionally held by men. But for women who make it into the corporate world, the opportunities are unbounded.

Gains for women are coming in every traditional male bastion. Women are entering law, medicine, business and engineering in huge numbers. Women make up approximately 54 percent of the U.S. workforce—almost 50 million women. In 1984 women represented over 15 percent of lawyers, almost 16 percent of doctors and over 32 percent of executives, managers and administrators. Additionally, women are opening their own businesses in record numbers. Companies owned by women now account for over $40 billion in sales. Women own over 3.5 million of the 13 million small U.S. businesses. This is a tremendous change from even ten years ago. Twenty years ago women didn't have more than a token representative in most occupations.

A number of significant factors have led to the growing participation and mobility in the workplace. One of the first major factors was the Civil Rights movement of the late 1950s and 1960s, which galvanized women into an awareness of the inequalities of our society. The publication of Betty Friedan's *The Feminine Mystique* applied these issues directly to the role of women. The popularity of the birth control pill in the 1960s led to a sexual revolution. Almost overnight, longstanding sexual taboos were thrown out. The 1960s was an era of protest. The Vietnam War was the first war in our country's history to be bitterly resisted by millions of people. At this same time, middle-class boys and girls began to experiment with hard and soft drugs in an unprecedented fashion. The 56 million "baby boomers" started to come of age in a society that was radically different from the late 1940s to late 1950s of their childhood. Additionally, the recession of the early 1970s forced women into the workplace in the largest numbers since World War II.

Young women, accustomed to protest and encouraged by loosening of traditional mores, began to demand equality. After the militant phase through which all protest movements pass, a quiet revolution began to take shape. Education became the greatest equalizer of all.

Women still have quite a way to go, as shown by a recent survey of graduating MBAs, who reported that men's attitudes toward women in management is as negative as it was the year before. But no matter what happens in the business and political climate, the gains that we have made will continue to increase.

There were a few women who had successful careers even before the women's movement of the 1970s. But these "queen bees" in the 1950s and early 1960s were considered oddities in a society that was still reeling from the repressive era of the 1950s. Even in 1965, I was discouraged from taking business courses, though I went to a predominantly business-oriented college.

Until recently many women who worked felt guilty about doing so. As a result, they tended to overcompensate. They often held two full-time jobs, their career and wife/mother. One woman told me of constantly having to justify her profession to the likes of the PTA and Cub Scouts. While these women had supportive husbands, they felt they had to do all the housework themselves. And when they were at work, they often felt they had to be totally on guard with their male colleagues. One woman said she was always afraid of seeming to be doing something a man wouldn't do, like saying that she had to leave early to go watch her child be an onion in a school play. Even today, many women executives still feel more comfortable saying they are leaving early to meet with their accountant than to accompany their child to an interview with the admissions director of a summer computer camp.

These early professional pioneers often took sabbaticals in their careers to have children. Today's professional women rarely fall off the fast track even if they have children. Many women return to their jobs after a short leave. Women today often postpone motherhood until they have established themselves in their careers. They are waiting until well past 30 to have their first child, a phenomenon virtually unheard of 20 years ago. Men are becoming much more actively involved in the parenting of children and in the general maintenance of the home.

The younger generation of men has been socialized to participate in running a home and rearing a family. This trend is due in part to people marrying later than they did a generation ago. The median age for first marriage is up and many men live by themselves before marriage. Men are therefore more accustomed to cooking, cleaning and taking care of themselves today whereas years ago men who went from mother to wife never needed to learn how to boil water. A generation ago professional women would abandon their careers if their husband had to relocate. Today it may be the husband who relocates if his wife gets a "too-good-to-pass-up" offer in a distant city.

Opportunities for women are beginning to open up in all areas. Women are entering business as well as government in unprecedented numbers. The 1984 Democratic party nominee for vice president, Geraldine Ferraro was the first woman to be nominated to national office by a major party. Sandra Day O'Connor is the first woman to sit on the Supreme Court. Jeane Kirkpatrick is the first woman to be U.S. Ambassador to the United Nations. Sally Ride and Judith Resnick were the first U.S. women astronauts.

In fact, women seem to have moved up faster in politics than in large corporations. Women hold only 5 percent of all executive positions. In the major corporations the percentage is even lower: Of 50,000 top executives only 1,000 are women and 49,000 are men. This is bound to change over time, however. The male executives now rising up the corporate ladder are much more comfortable with executive women than today's chief executive officers, because sometimes they are married to us.

Today only a relative handful of women are presidents, chief executive officers and chairmen of large corporations. But these numbers are growing. In Washington, D.C., the American Stock Exchange, Avon Products, Coca-Cola, Control Data, Esmark, Gulf Oil, Hallmark Cards, Hershey Foods and St. Joe Minerals all have lobbying offices headed by women executives. A recent dinner held at the American Stock Exchange in New York honored 150 prominent executive women who are top executives or owners of businesses earning over $5 million a year.

While the number of women in business and the professions is growing rapidly in the United States, most countries overseas are starting on the road to equality. Although women constitute 40 percent of Great Britain's labor force, they fill only 10 percent of its managerial posts. In 1984, however, in Switzerland where women were given the right to vote only 13 years ago, the Parliament chose a woman, Elisabeth Kopp, to be a cabinet minister for the first time in 136 years. Surprisingly, women hold 13 percent of managerial posts in Portugal, one of the poorer countries in Western Europe. Not surprisingly, women hold only 6 percent of managerial posts in Spain, a country that is still overwhelmingly macho.

A Ph.D. and European sales manager of a U.S. company sought venture capital funds to open her own computer company in London. She was repeatedly turned down by merchant bankers who felt that as a woman she would be unable to attract competent male professionals to work with her. She persevered and raised a then-British record of 2.1 million dollars for her startup. Olivetti, the giant Italian office equipment company, put up 25 percent. One progressive bank in Britain, National Westminster, is experimenting with a five-year program for women in management. They wisely reasoned that without this type of program that allows management women to take a leave for child raising, they were losing out on talented women who chose not to stay or didn't join the company in the first place.

In 1984, France's Socialist Prime Minister, Laurent Fabius, named Edwige Avice, 39, as the Secretary of State of the Defense Ministry in his Cabinet. In Germany, Petra Kelly, 36, is Nuremberg's Green Party representative to the German Parliament. In Italy, Maria Bellisario is the head of Italtel, the top telecommunications company. In Taiwan, Vivian Yen runs the Yue Loong Motor Company, one of the country's leading businesses.

While more opportunities for women in business and government are opening up in Western Europe, even countries in the Far East are beginning to see women advancing in the business world. As a result of rapidly growing industries such as electronics and textiles, women from rural areas in South Korea, Malaysia, Indonesia, the Philippines and Taiwan are flocking to the cities to work in factories. While this is only the beginning in a long process toward female careers, the increased literacy and later marriages that are resulting are providing the opportunity for young women to advance in the workforce.

Japan, with a highly educated female population, prepares women for professional careers that in the past haven't gone very far. Only one of the top 16 executives in the Japanese Federation of Electrical Machine workers is a woman, even though one fifth of the 530,000 members are female. In the technical and professional areas, a shortage of male software engineers has sent company recruiters increasingly to women's college campuses to seek women. Computer maker Fujitsu hired over 150 women software engineers in 1982. The high-technology industrial revolution constitutes one of the biggest fundamental changes affecting female careerism in Japan.

In the Middle East, progress for women, while slower than elsewhere, is still real. The majority of women have not even made the limited progress of Western Europe or the Far East; but the chief of the Saudi Press Agency in Washington, D.C., is a U.S.-educated Saudi Arabian woman. While few Middle Eastern women hold positions outside the home, this is slowly changing. Banks and other businesses owned by women, for women, are becoming increasingly popular in the Arab world.

In a number of the Latin American countries, particularly Argentina, Brazil, Uruguay and Chile, women are participating in the business world. In Colombia, the Minister for Communications, Noemi Sanin Posada is a young, well-educated, fairly high level governmental official.

In almost all the capitals of Latin America, young women office workers are a common sight. They work side by side with men up to levels of lower management. There are still few women in middle and upper management, except of course in family-owned businesses. Women as small business owners are becoming common. Recent improvements in literacy, the influence of feminism from the United States and Europe and a loosening of the traditional power of the church are beginning to make positive changes in the professional status of women in Latin America.

These gains and changes coming from all parts of the world are providing opportunities for U.S. women as never before. You will no longer be the first woman in a particular company office in a capacity other than secretary. Governments, corporations, small companies and schools are beginning to realize that women can do the job. It may still take twice the effort to get half the reward, but there is no question that the effort will lessen and the reward will increase. The more women in business and politics worldwide, the easier it will become to penetrate areas where women were previously excluded.

WHY INTERNATIONAL?

"I am having a hard enough time getting ahead in a domestic company," you may say to me. "Why should I take on the added fight of dealing with foreigners who are even more resistant to women?"

The answer is that international business is the field of the twenty-first century. There will be more opportunities for women in global business, because the international sector is growing, the rules are changing and the pace is faster.

The great industrial might of the United States went unchallenged for many years. The internal market could absorb all the output of our industries, and our natural resources were so seemingly abundant that we didn't need to import raw materials.

But while U.S. industry ignored foreign markets, other countries, especially Japan and West Germany, began to see that the road to higher profits and production ran across national boundaries.

Japan's small size, and Germany's proximity to other European nations, forced these countries to be exporters. Japanese and German executives are old hands at dealing with foreign trade partners. The United States, on the other hand, is incredibly naïve when it comes to international matters. Leonard A. Lauder, president and CEO of the cosmetics company Estée Lauder, once said that if we could get people to understand that not everyone in the world speaks English, we'd eliminate half of the U.S. trade deficit.

In 1984, that trade deficit broke all records at $120 billion. Some of this had to do with the incredible strength of the dollar, which makes it easier for us to buy foreign goods than for people overseas to buy U.S.-made products. Another factors is the debt situation of the developing world. U.S. executives also complain about various forms of protectionism, which they claim unfairly keep our goods out of many foreign markets. But a significant part of the problem has to do with the simple fact that most U.S. executives simply don't know how to do business with foreign executives.

This lack of understanding, combined with a serious dose of ethnocentrism, has cost U.S. companies millions of dollars. We still try to sell our lefthand-drive cars to countries where people drive on the left side of the road and need righthand steering. Up till recently, advertisements for refrigerators in the Middle East could be found depicting the shelves full of ham, while the refrigerator companies wondered why Moslems (who are forbidden to eat pork) bought refrigerators from West Germany or Japan.

The stories of marketing blunders are legion. General Motors test marketed the Chevrolet Nova in Latin American markets, not considering that *no va* means "it doesn't go" in Spanish. The campaign bombed spectacularly. Less well-known blunders include the large multinational corporation that attempted to sell baby food in an African nation by using the same labels as in the U.S. market, which showed a picture of a baby. African consumers took a look at the product and were horrified: They thought from the labels that the jars contained ground-up babies. Pillsbury's Jolly Green Giant was originally translated literally as the "intimidating green ogre" in Saudi Arabia. Later a more liberal translation produced the "Giant of the Valley," which no doubt sold more vegetables.

Many foreign companies have taken over markets that once were ours, not only because their products are superior or even less expensive, but because they know how to sell to consumers who don't share their language and culture.

U.S. companies tried in the past to sell products overseas that had been designed for the U.S. market, instead of researching what kind of products overseas consumers wanted. We made top-loading washing machines, so we tried to export top-loading washing machines. No one seemed to pay attention to the fact that women in Latin America, who tend to be shorter than women in the United States, are more comfortable with front-loading washing machines. When any effort at all was made to accommodate our products to overseas markets, it was by "retrofitting"—taking a finished product and tinkering with it to make it acceptable to overseas consumers. No one ever thought of designing a new product with a foreign market in mind.

Even when U.S. products were suitable for export, and weren't advertised in a way that turned off their intended consumer, many sales were lost because the managers responsible for selling them didn't speak the language of the buyers or didn't understand international negotiating. In many cases, the only thing American companies exported was their markets, which were taken over by foreign producers who made products designed with their customers' cultures in mind and who understood how to "massage" their negotiating partners.

All of this has begun to change, largely because U.S. executives' lack of intercultural understanding has hurt their companies right in the bottom line. Change is coming slowly, but old beliefs hold on. Twenty years ago, when worldwide competition wasn't so fierce, U.S. goods were unanimously regarded as the best in the world. Nobody then would have thought of buying Japanese goods for their quality. All that is reversed now, and U.S. companies are trying hard to catch up. Business schools are just beginning to realize the importance of international negotiating and a few of the more sophisticated and progressive schools have initiated courses on the subject.

Today the extent of global competition is such that U.S. companies are beginning to become much more flexible and global in their strategic planning. Many U.S. companies are shifting their manufacturing activity abroad. Some big companies are giving up production of key products to foreign companies altogether and are acting as marketing agents. Some companies are attempting to cut costs by buying cheaper foreign-made components whenever possible. The United States has become the leading importer of foreign goods. U.S. imports were valued at over $335 billion in 1984.

Exporting has become more and more difficult, except in industries where a new technology is in demand and price is not an issue. Even in these cases the competition is strong from other industrialized nations. Price is less of an issue when long-term relationships between seller and buyer exist. In many countries throughout the world no business is conducted, no matter what the price is, unless a personal relationship exists. Developing these relationships is time-consuming and costly, but the expense is preferable to doing no business at all.

It's ironic that in an era of depersonalizing electronic communications, the face-to-face meeting and the handshake to seal the transaction are more important than ever. As the economic recovery gathers steam, opportunities for trade will come from all corners of the world. U.S. executives, if savvy in international negotiating, will see a big demand for their products and services in the Far East, Western Europe and Latin America. We are beginning to see more combinations of global joint ventures, deals, mergers, trades and countertrades than ever before. This is likely to continue for a long time, providing unlimited opportunities in the international marketplace. Women who know their industry and learn to negotiate are the best candidates to succeed in these overseas ventures.

2

Preparing for Your Career in International Business

How do you prepare yourself properly for a career in international business? There are two basic paths that you can choose. One is to pick an area of business, such as marketing, finance, management or whatever interests you, study for it, practice it domestically, and when you are quite competent in your field, learn about how to apply it in the international arena. The other is to begin thinking internationally when you begin to prepare for your career.

In a world that is shrinking rapidly even as it is growing more competitive, you're better off thinking internationally at the outset. But if you have already prepared yourself for a career in domestic business, you can become knowledgeable about the international side of your specialty within a short time. Many U.S. companies already have multinational, international or "global" operations in which you can apply the skills you have already practiced in the domestic division. The United States is also host to hundreds of foreign companies that need skilled managers to run their American subsidiaries. Both of these trends will continue for the long term.

Training for a career in international business could begin as early as grade school with the study of foreign languages. Not all of us are lucky enough to get such an early start. But certainly by the time a young person who aspires to a career in international business is in college, a portion of the curriculum should be devoted to one or more foreign languages and to other international studies.

As the world is shrinking, so is the need for generalists in management. You simply cannot "specialize" in international business alone; you must acquire hard skills in a growing area, such as marketing, sales, accounting, finance, computer science, law or engineering. You can then apply these skills to the international field.

International courses should be taken as a minor, or even better, as a co-major on the undergraduate or graduate business school level. These course areas might include: International Trade and Finance, International Marketing, International Economics, Legal and Tax Aspects of International Business, and so on. These courses, which are taught in most business schools, are all very important. However, perhaps the most important subject, International Business Negotiating, is taught in only a handful of schools, such as the University of Pennsylvania and New York University. While not specifically international in scope, any courses on sales and entrepreneurship are also valuable as they focus on the personal and motivational aspects of business. These skills are vital in an international business career.

If you have already finished your education, it may not be necessary to go back to school to get another college degree. However, if you are not already experienced in the international marketplace, I recommend that you take at least some courses or seminars, or even a certificate program in some aspect of international business. Many universities offer excellent programs in the Continuing Education or Extension divisions. For example, in the Fall of 1985, I chaired a seminar at New York University's School of Continuing Education called "Conducting Business in the World Marketplace: New Opportunities for Women." The course attracted 31 women representing every area of domestic business. It was so well received that it will be offered again in the Fall of 1986.

If you are still in school, international expertise is not hard to acquire today, as almost all business schools now have international tracks. Many law schools offer programs including multinational business transactions and taxation, and in comparative law (studying the legal systems of other countries). Many schools of government and public administration also offer international programs.

Of the 1984 class at NYU's Graduate School of Business Administration approximately 50 percent are women, and 20 percent of these women are studying in an international business concentration along with their finance, marketing, computer or accounting tracks. In the survey, 52 percent of these women indicated that they would relocate for advancement and 43 percent said they would travel frequently for business. Their attitudes indicate a growing trend toward interest in international business.

Additionally, there are schools that specialize in the international (management) field such as the American Graduate School of International Management (better known as Thunderbird), in Arizona. Over 300 schools in every part of the United States have some form of international program.*

While some of these schools offer only a few international courses, the majority of schools offer undergraduate business degrees with a concentration or major in international finance, management, marketing or economics. Many of these schools also offer masters degree programs and some have doctoral programs in international business. While these programs are by no means uniform or standardized, there are enough schools in every region for you to choose a recognized program.

A number of schools also offer internships overseas or study abroad courses. If time and money are not barriers, you should by all means enroll in these programs, to get some direct experience with a foreign language and culture.

When you graduate, you may be fortunate enough to find a job in a corporation that will train you for international business. But don't look only for international jobs at the beginning of your career, even if you have concentrated on international courses in business school. You can always practice your specialty domestically for a while and then go international. One way to get experience is to find a company that will allow you to be an unpaid intern. In this way, you learn all you can in a short period of time and parlay that knowledge into a salaried position at that company or another.

The job of transition to, or entry into, international business is easier if you already have the requisite "soft skills." If you are already a manager or executive in a domestic operation, take some courses in international business and then learn about a particular area of the world and its culture. You are then ready to apply for a transfer or a new job in an international division. If you are a woman who is just beginning a business career, consider management traineeships. If you are still in school, try to find summer internships in international divisions of U.S. corporations, in foreign firms or with import-export companies. The pay may be low (or nonexistent), but the exposure could be just the thing to get you hired after you graduate. Management traineeships in large international companies and banks are another way to get valuable experience. For women who are entering a second career in business, after a "traditional" career such as social work,

---

*A comprehensive list of these schools was published in August 1981 in *Business America*, a Department of Commerce publication.

teaching or nursing, an internship or traineeship program may make the transition to international business easier than you'd think.

Combine your communication or "people skills" with some "hard" international and management skills and some cultural and language training, and take an entry-level job to start. One former high school language teacher took a low-paying job in an international sales organization, and worked her way up to one of the top sales jobs in the company.

Many women are still reluctant to be aggressive when it comes to their careers and feel that they will eventually be recognized for their ability. This attitude, like other old myths, is falling by the wayside. In international as well as domestic business, the way to succeed is to learn a skill, develop a confident personality (even if you have to fake confidence at first) and gain total expertise in the products or service you are selling. But once you have achieved this foundation, you must be assertive and push for the assignments you want and for the promotions you deserve. Quietly waiting for recognition won't do it anymore (if it ever did). Become visible in your field. Write articles and give speeches. It's the best way to promote yourself. Join organizations and network your way into new jobs.

If you are considering changing careers or returning to the workplace, the international field may be the place for you. Age is not a handicap here. In fact, in many countries throughout the world, older really *is* better. Certain cultures venerate age and may be more willing to listen to an older person.

While women are not yet totally accepted in all areas of business, whether domestic or international, there is widespread agreement that women are often better than men at negotiation. Women are generally more verbal and flexible. They tend to view the negotiating process as part of a long-term relationship. Because these skills of patient negotiating are so vital in an international setting, a 45- to 50-year-old woman with "hard" professional skills may often be the best candidate to negotiate a high-powered international deal!

The only other thing such a woman would need to succeed in the international arena is a strong background in "soft" or cultural skills. In our culture, women have been socialized from early childhood to be more dependent on others. Therefore, it is often easier for a woman to understand and internalize the importance of culture in the international marketplace. In contrast, there are men who still believe that the "soft skills" are not necessary when doing business overseas, much to the detriment of the bottom line of their companies.

Cross-cultural skills can be learned both by face-to-face experience and through research or schooling. If you vacation in other countries, try to learn something of the culture and lifestyle of the local population. Observe people at their daily tasks. This may not be sufficient for a career in international business but it's certainly a start. If you have an interest in a particular region, focus on it. I say region, because it is best to specialize in a region rather than a country to maximize your professional opportunities. Be sure to learn the differences between countries in that region. Argentina is as different from Brazil as Italy is from France.

Learning a foreign language is one of the most important cultural skills you can acquire. The Japanese and many Western Europeans are amazed at how few Americans know other languages. Few U.S. colleges still require foreign language study. It is simply not seen as what it is—a requirement for global competitiveness in business. The U.S. position in foreign trade needs all the edge it can get. Our narrow-minded attitude toward foreign language can best be summed up by a congressman who opposed a bill to provide $150 million in grants for teaching foreign languages when he declared, "If Jesus Christ spoke English, it's good enough for me."

Americans *must* learn foreign languages unless we want to continue abandoning our export markets to the Japanese, Germans and others. Many international executives from all parts of the world speak fluent English and have at least a passing knowledge of the culture of the United States. Approximately 95 percent of the Japanese who do business in the United States speak English. In contrast, only perhaps 1 percent of Americans doing business in Japan speak Japanese.

Many Americans have language-learning fears similar to the well-known "math fear." While it is ideal to learn a foreign language before puberty, there is no reason why you can't learn a foreign language with some skill at any time in your life. There are literally hundreds of language programs offered in most large cities, from inexpensive group classes to individual total immersion courses. Records, tapes and books are an inexpensive way to begin learning or to refresh your knowledge of a language. In many large cities, there are also foreign language programs on radio and TV.

There are any number of ways to learn the language and the culture of a country or region. In many cities there are associations such as the Brazilian American Society, Japan House, Goethe House (German) and the Alliance Française, which offer the opportunity to learn a language and converse with native speakers. These organizations sponsor not only language classes, but also cultural seminars, social events, cooking classes and trips to restaurants, museums and movies, all of which can help you to learn not only the language of a foreign country but also its cuisine, social customs, literature and history.

In addition most large cities have foreign-owned restaurants, foreign-language movie theaters and stores that carry magazines and newspapers in foreign languages. If you live in any large city you can eat a different ethnic cuisine every night for at least a month! Learning a foreign language and culture is not necessarily easy but can certainly be enjoyable.

Some of the languages and cultures most in demand in international business today are Japanese, Arabic and Chinese. These languages are particularly difficult to learn for Americans, as are their cultures. French, Spanish and German are also still extremely important languages to learn for international business and they are somewhat easier to learn because they are written in the familiar Roman alphabet and because many words in these languages are closely related to English words. Also, the cultures of European countries are more familiar to most of us than the cultures of Asia or the Middle East.

While you do not necessarily need to speak a language fluently in order to have successful careers, you will increase your chances overseas if you speak another language at least passably.

There is no way to learn everything about another culture except by living in it for a good deal of time. But you *must* learn the most important points. Literally millions of dollars in business have been lost by American businessmen who didn't observe the most fundamental rules of another culture, and alienated their foreign hosts. Such acts as using the left (bathroom) hand or showing the sole of the shoe in Arabic society, looking a Japanese contact deeply in the eyes, touching an Asian or recoiling in horror at being hugged or kissed by a Latin or Arab are the best-known examples of offensive ignorance. Many far more subtle mistakes made by Americans cost dearly. Impatience in negotiating—what we see as wanting to "put the cards on the table"—is seen in almost all other cultures as rude and boorish.

Another very important idea in conducting international business is the variable concept of time. Many cultures throughout the world view time differently from Americans. In the United States, a meeting set for 10:00 A.M. will begin no later than 10:15. In some parts of the world, it may begin hours later. In Mexico, local executives will often jokingly specify whether the time set for a meeting is *hora mexicana* or *hora americana*.

To do business in other countries you must get to know your contact or host. Without this personal familiarity negotiations will never be taken seriously. We in the United States do a great deal of business on the telephone, through the mail and in other impersonal ways. Overseas, nothing will ever replace the face-to-face meeting. It is not uncommon for us to call someone by his or her first name over the phone or at a first meeting. This will not work in most foreign countries. To conduct serious business overseas, a long-term relationship of trust must be established.

Most Americans find it very difficult to attend "meetings" where little or no business is discussed. They see this process as a waste of time and therefore boring or think they are being put off. Nothing could be further from the truth! Your hosts are trying to get an understanding of who you are as a person, before they will commit themselves to negotiating the terms of the business deal.

Be prepared, and prepare those to whom you report, to spend a good deal of time without immediate gratification (that is, sales made). Relationships must be cultivated over a period of time. This is easier for women than for many men. Traditionally, women have been brought up to be patient. Another vital concept in dealing with many other countries is that of family relationships. The extended family (almost unknown in the United States today) is the focus of social life in many areas, particularly in Latin American and Arabic cultures. The welfare of these family members may come before the scheduled meeting with you. Broken or postponed appointments can occur in these cultures and again women (even in sexist Arabic countries) have somewhat of an edge in dealing with these problems. Concern for family members has, up until recently, been the responsibility of women in American society. Your tolerance of these and other ambiguous norms will result in gaining acceptance and trust. The time spent allowing your client to get to know you will be well worth it when you come back to your home office, a signed contract in hand!

3

Careers in International Business

In today's business world, the road to the executive suite often passes through the international division. In a 1979 poll of Fortune 500 executives (both male and female) almost 70 percent said that international experience is a requirement for promotion to top management. These executives agreed that international experience is especially important in a company whose CEO is in charge of both domestic and international operations. More than half said that international experience would be important even in selecting the head of a purely *domestic* division.

As recently as six or seven years ago, very few women were in international positions, whether stationed overseas or traveling from a home-office base. While the percentage of expatriate women managers is still fairly low, the number of women traveling overseas on business is booming.

Since women are entering every type of career domestically, areas of international business that were previously male-dominated are also opening up. This pressure on corporations results from equal opportunity legislation, from women's high levels of education and (most of all) from the tremendous drive on the part of women, which has produced gains in domestic responsibility as well as in the international sector. Many major corporations are rethinking their policies and have realized that unless women can advance and grow in their careers, both the women and the corporations stand to lose. The enormous pool of high-quality talent represented by women in the workforce has had a positive effect on the economic situation in the United States, especially at the higher end. In families with income between $40,000 and $50,000, 70 percent of the women now hold jobs.

Women are now requesting overseas posts and positions requiring frequent travel, because we know that that is the way to the executive suite. The place that women must do the most convincing is not overseas, where initial resistance can be broken down, but in the home office.

For some women stationed overseas, managing in a foreign country may be less of a problem than the resistance from the home office, where top management is very sensitive to what foreigners think of a woman. Until recently, most male executives simply assumed that foreign businessmen were accustomed to more male-dominated cultures and would be resistant to doing business with women from the United States. However, most foreign businessmen are no more reluctant to doing business with an American woman than with an American man. In 1981 Xerox Corporation's China operation was headed by a woman. SUNOCO Overseas (a subsidiary of Sun Oil Co.) and Southeast First National Bank of Miami both have women heading their operations in Latin America. Women also head up General Electric in Moscow and Bank of America in Tokyo and Beijing. These are just a few examples of postings that would have been unthinkable ten years ago, but are increasingly common today. Women *can* function well in business, even in the most macho cultures.

This is not to say that the picture for women is altogether wonderful. (Is it ever?) Women are still underrepresented in international business on all levels, but are making superb gains. Unfortunately, with all the lip service given about professional quality in the United States, there are still a lot of unliberated males in upper levels of management. These are the people who must be shown and convinced that qualified women can not only match the performance of males overseas, but can far exceed them in almost all international business ventures.

In a 1984 Gallup poll of almost 500 female executives, only 35 percent reported spending five days a month traveling for business. Even women in domestic positions reported the same problem: management fears that even U.S. businessmen won't deal with U.S. businesswomen on an equal footing.

Of course, many of these fears about how "someone else" will react to women managers are only expressions of a male boss's own sexist attitudes. Projecting these antifeminist feelings onto these unseen "others" is a (conscious or subconscious) way of making a male executive's sexist feelings seem more acceptable to himself or his subordinates. (Of course, the courts have held in many cases under the equal employment opportunity laws that resistance by a company's customers to doing business with women is no excuse for the company to deny women equality in hiring, training or promotions.)

The way to overcome these attitudes is to confront the issue with the person(s) in charge, request travel responsibility and prove that you can succeed. If your efforts are resisted, ask for reasons and attempt to enlighten management when all the old dinosaurs are presented. Support your argument with facts about women who have succeeded overseas, and ask for a chance to prove yourself.

There are industries that have traditionally promoted women and have moved them into positions of prominence more easily than others. Women have gained overseas experience in publishing, banking and retailing, probably because there have been many women in the domestic branches of these industries for many years. Women in these fields have moved into positions of international responsibility faster than in other industries, because of their already greater numbers and visibility in the home offices.

But what about all the other industries? If you already work in a large multinational corporation, bank, insurance company, consulting firm, advertising agency or accounting firm, and want to get into the international field, you may have the opportunity within your own company. Almost all large U.S. corporations have either an overseas subsidiary, an international division or branch or at least some overseas clients or suppliers.

If you work in a smaller company that deals only with domestic clients, you will have to change to a company within your field that is international in scope. If you are not already settled in a career, be sure to look for jobs with international potential, but don't turn down a solely domestic job if it is in your area of expertise. You can always change employers after you've gotten some solid domestic experience. It's often said that a good sales rep can sell anything. It's equally true that a good sales rep can sell any *where*.

If you're not already established in a particular field, one of the best places to look for a career is within a service industry. The U.S. economy is rapidly becoming service-oriented. While manufacturing is declining, the service sector already accounts for three quarters of total U.S. employment. From May to October 1984, the service sector alone accounted for 85 percent of the growth in total nonfarm employment. Gains in service jobs averaged *170,000* per month in July, August and September of 1984. Even in postrecessionary 1984, a wide range of industries supplying business and consumer services, such as advertising, consulting and hotels, reported their best business in years. In large cities throughout the United States, service companies are becoming the largest employers. Over the next ten years, six out of seven new jobs will be in services.

This trend is also true internationally. The international market of "invisible" (that is, service) trade is estimated at $700 billion annually!

The fields of banking, publishing and retailing, which are front runners for women in international business, are all service-related industries. I participated in a recent seminar at New York University called "American Women: Distinguished International Careers," with seven other women in the fields of marketing, banking, retailing, executive recruiting, investments, government, consulting and education. We represented a cross-section of international careers in service industries and explained the huge potential for women in these fields.

Perhaps the fastest track to the top corporate executive jobs is in sales and marketing. In a 1984 survey taken by Heidrick and Struggles, an international executive search firm, almost a third of the CEOs of non-industrial (service) firms had backgrounds in marketing or sales.

While marketing and sales jobs are closely related, they often have very different career paths. Traditionally, there are a set number of steps up the corporate ladder within the consumer marketing arena. These may include assistant product manager, associate product manager, product manager, brand manager, marketing manager, director of marketing, marketing vice president, and so on. In small corporations, one or more of these steps may be omitted. In sales, on the other hand, there is no such direct hierarchy, but there may still be many steps to the top levels. It is occasionally difficult for a salesperson to cross over into management, but many salespeople prefer to stay out of management because of the flexibility and challenge they find in direct selling.

Related to marketing and sales are the fields of advertising and market research. These two areas have literally exploded in the international arena. With all the debate about "global" advertising and "world brands," international advertising and market research have opened up significantly. Women have traditionally been fairly visible in both advertising and marketing research, but for many years were concentrated at the lower end. For example, advertising women were frequently stuck at the account executive level. Recently, women have begun to emerge in small but growing numbers as vice presidents and creative directors. Women have also been extremely successful as owners of their own advertising agencies. The demand for high-quality marketing research has created top-level positions in the market research companies as well as internal departments in corporations.

In smaller companies, while the pay may not be as high as in the large corporations, a marketing/salesperson may get more visibility early on. For those who don't care to go through the traditional steps of consumer and bank marketing, a job with a smaller company may be the way to move up quickly. You might take a marketing position in a small domestic or international company, gain visibility and experience for a few years and then move on to a larger international-oriented company and circumvent years of small hop-steps.

Sales experience is a transferable skill. If you are a strong closer, you can parlay that experience into the international sales market whether you're selling shoes or capital equipment.

There is still some residual reluctance on the part of women to go into direct sales as a career because of the bad press given to salesmen in years past. Fortunately, salespersons have become a good deal more sophisticated and educated in the recent past. Almost gone are the days of the pinky-ringed, white-belted, white-patent-leather-shoed salesmen. One of the most successful car salespersons in the United States is a woman. "Sales executives," as they are now called with their higher levels of education, sell everything from sophisticated financial "products" to intangible services. Many college graduates feel they don't need an education for sales or that sales is not what they were trained for. Nevertheless, sales is an excellent place to learn quickly and efficiently how to negotiate business deals. While you must be internationally savvy to negotiate sales overseas, it doesn't take an advanced degree to learn a language and culture. Sales experience, cultural knowledge and communication skills are all you need to succeed. If you feel you have the aptitude for sales, don't be reluctant to try this field.

In a recent survey, 40 women at a seminar in international marketing said that contacts and interpersonal relationships are the most important factors for success in international marketing. Previous work experience, speaking a foreign language, formal education and willingness to move were rated next most important.

The second most common backgrounds in the executive suite are finance and accounting, representing more than one fourth of the CEOs surveyed in the Heidrick and Struggles study. The most common entry-level position in finance is financial analyst at a commercial or investment bank. Traditionally, analysts then move through the ranks of lower and middle management, much the way the consumer goods marketer does. There is a lot of money to be made in investment banking, particularly if you manage the assets of wealthy individuals or corporations, here or abroad. While women have only recently begun to reach vice president and higher levels, there is definitely a trend toward more women in investment banking. With the influx of foreign capital into the United States, as foreign investors seek high interest rates and a stable political climate, the international positions in investment banking are now more numerous than ever. Today, women hold more than 53 percent of all professional posts in the top banks.

Women have always had a fairly strong presence in commercial banking and are beginning to emerge in high positions in international lending. Training in credit and skill at negotiating are the major requisites for high-level jobs as international lenders or commercial loan workout specialists.

Accounting has seen a huge influx of women in the United States in the past 15 years. There are now close to 500,000 female accountants, or 39 percent of the nation's accountants, compared with only 160,000 in 1970. While the most highly sought-after jobs are in the big eight accounting firms, many smaller firms also have international clients. The most obvious choices for finance and accounting professionals are banks, brokerage firms and accounting firms, but there is also a tremendous amount of opportunity in small, medium and large corporations in all industries for women with these skills.

The information explosion has opened up a vast array of jobs in computer and information sciences, commonly known as "MIS" (management information science). This area includes opportunities from entry-level data-processing to executive-level managerial positions. Companies in all industries are automating their operations with amazing rapidity. All forms of communications jobs offer extremely fast-changing careers, and because this is a relatively new field, it shows great promise for women to advance.

Today 19 percent of engineering students and almost 40 percent of technical students are women. Only 10 percent of high-tech managers are women, but this is sure to increase. There is still some difficulty in finding women who have both management and technical skills, but that is changing rapidly. While 12 percent of the CEOs currently come from the engineering field, the influx of computer, communications and information companies will cause sharp increases in that number in the 1990s.

The 22 percent of CEOs that come out of manufacturing/operations probably never thought that women would encroach on their territory. While women have traditionally stayed away from these line jobs, women now make up 40 percent of technical students and are beginning to make their presence felt.

The broad areas known as management and administration are somewhat difficult to pin down. According to the Census Bureau, the percentage of women employed as management analysts increased from 25 percent in 1970 to 45 percent in 1980. This statistic includes the traditional women's areas such as personnel, human resources, employee benefits and pensions and general staff administration. While somewhat downgraded in the past, these areas are beginning to take on new importance as the more glamorous organizational behavior professionals with graduate and doctoral degrees enter these fields. The quality of work life and productivity have become major issues in corporations throughout the United States.

But perhaps the greatest opportunity may be in owning your own business and taking it into the international sector. More than 3.5 million women in the United States own their own businesses, which generate over $40 billion a year. Over 45 percent of these businesses are in service—the great strength of our economy. Women are often opening their own businesses because, like the immigrants to the United States earlier in this century, they are finding that it can be the fastest route into the mainstream. While a good percentage of these women-owned businesses are small, these women's drive and ambition are huge, and so is the success that follows!

Don't overlook the many state, local and federal government jobs that are international in scope. A short stint in an international government job can be a short cut to rapid promotion when you return to the private sector. These are also some very satisfying long-term international careers in the government sector. For example, in the International Trade Administration of the Department of Commerce, there are jobs such as trade specialist in district offices, Foreign Commercial Service Officer, International Economist, Desk Officer and Trade Promotion Specialist. Eximbank and OPIC (Overseas Private Investment Corporation) employ bankers and economists. The Agency for International Development (AID) and the State Department employ economists and investment development specialists. The United States Information Agency (USIA) hires officers to develop programs for visiting executives and diplomats.

Other career opportunities exist in Chambers of Commerce, trade associations, export trading and export management companies, and in multinational organizations such as the UN and the International Monetary Fund, to name a few.

Law also offers many good opportunities for international careers. Over 8 percent of the CEOs of major corporations currently come from legal backgrounds. A very good way for women to leapfrog the lower and middle levels of management is to become a lawyer, practice corporate law for a while and then enter upper levels of management. There is still a somewhat intimidating quality to being a lawyer, and women lawyers are frequently good at negotiating. In international business, this is a tremendous plus, and as a lawyer you will enter the corporate world with built-in status. If you chose to practice international law, there are many well-regarded international firms throughout the United States that deal almost exclusively with overseas clients or with the foreign legal problems of U.S. clients.

No matter what field you choose, the only limit to your success is your drive and imagination.

4

Doing Business in the World Marketplace: An Introduction to International Negotiating

The United States of America is the greatest market in the world. With over 230 million people, 3,000 miles between coasts and a high standard of living, business opportunities are unlimited. Or so we in the United States thought until recently. Because of the great internal demand, there was little incentive to aggressively seek out business from other countries. Business came to us from all over the world.

Things have changed dramatically, and while the United States is still the leader in many industrial and non-industrial sectors, quality competition is coming fast from all over the world. U.S. business is slowly beginning to realize that in order to continue being profitable, it has to focus more effort in overseas markets.

Since the dollar has been so strong, imported goods have been flooding the U.S. market. The U.S. competitive position is shaky within the United States and overseas as well. Japan alone has 17 percent of the U.S. car market.

Business is waking up to the fact that foreign competition is here to stay. U.S. industry used to think it could compete simply on a quality platform. We thought that because our goods were better than anyone else's, the world would come to us and we wouldn't have to market to them. Those days are over. In almost every industry one or more foreign producers matches or surpasses our goods for quality or price. The Japanese make better and cheaper television sets, the West Germans make better cars, Brazil exports cheaper steel and the Swiss make better chocolate.

Because U.S. products can no longer compete successfully solely on quality or price, management is beginning to realize that the key to success in the global marketing is in the *selling*.

To sell successfully you must first know your market. For a manager born and raised in the United States it is sometimes hard to recognize that consumers in Milan or Mecca have cultures vastly different from consumers in Minneapolis or Malibu.

The United States is a young country and Americans pride themselves on having a democratic culture, with few class-based distinctions. Americans have no royal family and do not confer titles of nobility. We are not usually defined by our ancestry. While regional differences may be great, most Americans tend to minimize these differences and view themselves as being similar to people in the rest of the United States.

This accounts for the breezy, informal nature of doing business within the United States. It is not uncommon for a businessperson to call a new contact 3,000 miles away and begin first-naming during the first five minutes of the conversation. This practice is almost never regarded as insulting, but as an easy way to avoid wading through hours of getting to know each other. Even in complex deals, managers and executives in the United States often do not meet face-to-face until they are ready to close the deal.

Many foreign cultures are more formal, and their societies are more stratified. In most other countries, there is a greater emphasis on polite, or even courtly, manners. Nothing gets done without many face-to-face meetings first. When businesspeople meet overseas, it is usually to open negotiations and to begin a long and complex relationship.

The failure to recognize these differences in culture, and the resulting differences in styles of doing business, costs U.S. industry millions of dollars each year in lost sales and lost opportunities.

In practically all countries throughout the world, but most importantly in the Middle East, Latin America and the Far East, no business is conducted until and unless a foundation of trust has been set. This rule applies to any deal larger than selling a 79-cent replacement widget. Very little business is concluded through letters, calls or telexes. These impersonal-type communications may be a good way to start a relationship, but only a series of sit-down meetings will result in the closing of any deal.

In overseas business one will almost never hear a conversation like this typical U.S. phone call:

"Interstellar computer."

"Hello, may I speak to Barbara Smith? This is Pat Collins of American Biz Company in New York. How's the weather in Los Angeles?"

"Oh, it's sunny and warm, what's it like in New York?"

"Cloudy and cold, Barbara, it's January. I understand that you are in the market for a software program for your telecommunications satellite. I have the perfect program for your operation."

"We usually get all our software from HiPrice Company, which is here in Malibu, Pat."

"Well, Barbara, I think we can beat their price and I'll send you our price list, a sample program and specifications."

"Fine, Pat, I'd like to see them."

"OK, call me when you get the information."

"Will do. Bye."

A week later:

"Hello, American Biz Company."

"Pat Collins, please."

"Pat Collins here."

"Hi, Pat, Barbara Smith here, how are you?"

"Just great. We read your price list and we'd like to order your Starpak."

"That's wonderful, I knew it was just right for Interstellar."

"I'll send you a check today."

"That's terrific, good talking to you."

"Bye-bye."

Doing business in this manner is common within the United States. This negotiating style is unique to this country. Although on the surface, the dialogue sounds informal and spontaneous, the people involved are responding to a well-choreographed, culturally determined set of cues. While this style would never work overseas, a heavy-handed, more formal and long-winded presentation would be a disaster in the United States, whether on the telephone or in person. The interchange works well because it is based on a series of accepted standards. Pat Collins doesn't really care about the weather 3,000 miles away in Los Angeles, but the inquiry immediately establishes a feeling of camaraderie. Angelinos are personally proud of their unrelentingly sunny weather, while New Yorkers seem to take a perverse pleasure in continually griping about their weather. Briefly discussing the weather is a successful sales tool, because it allows the buyer and seller to create a feeling of friendship.

This feeling is an illusion, of course. Neither woman *really* cares what the weather is like 3,000 miles away, and it is unlikely that they will ever even speak to each other again after this deal is over, much less meet face to face. But creating the appearance of friendship is important in our culture.

(If both women were in the same city or region, the caller would begin with some other pleasantry.)

The caller next says that American Biz Co. knows that Interstellar is interested in software. It is obvious that she has done her homework. How did ABC know that Interstellar was buying software? Barbara Smith probably won't ask. Pat Collins smoothly assures her that ABC has *the perfect* program for her at a lower price than the competition. Price and quality are the selling points that count in our culture. Long-term relationships to establish trust are unnecessary for selling in the United States. Quality is fairly standard, and since competition is strong there is little reason to continue with a supplier if another one can provide a good product at the right price.

Nor is a personal relationship with a customer or a supplier necessary. Often it is not even possible; America is a very mobile society and people do not stay in the same place or job for a long time. Promotions within a company, changes to other companies and moves to other parts of the country are frequent. There are few patterns of family ties and friendship to produce relationships with inefficient suppliers.

In many regions of the world personal relationships are the only basis for doing business. In some countries this practice has been carried to the extreme, and has produced widespread inefficiency and control of business by a few interlocking families. In other countries, while business is not controlled by a small group, few foreign suppliers will be able to penetrate the market without a long series of getting-to-know-you meetings. Although it is not always necessary to have a contact already in place, it certainly can speed up the negotiating process.

Negotiations in the United States, even those that involve large sums of money, have to do with agreeing on price and terms. In other parts of the world, negotiations are simply the beginning of a long process. A senior minister of Japan's Ministry of International Trade and Industry (MITI) advises, "to really get access to [Japan's] market, you've got to learn the language and drink sake in nightclubs for three or four years. Can you find many American executives delighted to do this?" This long process may seem ridiculous to an American manager or executive who thinks only of the short-term bottom line. But the Japanese market is well worth the long-term investment, and U.S. businesses are beginning to learn how to get into it.

If you are beginning to cultivate contacts overseas, ask your business acquaintances in the United States if they know anyone in that country or region. Very often, just knowing a name in a particular country can help you. Better yet is a letter of introduction to a contact. This type of introduction is a highly effective way to cut down on long hours of establishing your credibility.

If you work for a large company, you can reduce introduction formalities in a number of ways. First, if your company is well known, its name alone is often enough to establish your credibility and to open some doors. Second, a large company often has branches, subsidiaries, or production facilities in place overseas. Third, given the globalism of large companies, they often have foreign nationals working in the U.S. headquarters office who can refer you to friends or business contacts in their country.

If you work for a small company and don't have any contacts already established overseas, begin corresponding with the person you will be meeting. At least three or four months before you meet, you should be writing regularly, telexing, and calling if not prohibitively expensive. Letters should include brochures about your company and its products, polite inquiries about your contact's company, some brief biographical information on your professional history, an expression of interest in your contact's "beautiful" country and other low-key pleasantries.

All well and good, you may say, but what if you just found out that you're going to Zagreb next week? Make quick inquiries to your business friends in the United States to find out if they know anyone at all in Yugoslavia. Next, call or wire the person you're going to meet immediately. Explain the reason for your hastily scheduled meeting and apologize for not having more time to prepare.

The reason that correspondence should begin in advance of your meeting is to start developing a long-term relationship of trust. In most cases, deals aren't made nor are contracts signed at the first face-to-face meeting. If you have established in advance the fact that you are a woman (not all people in foreign countries will be able to know from your name whether you are a man or a woman), you will make it easier at the first meeting. Your contact may have no problem doing business with you, but he may be surprised at seeing a woman if he thought he would be meeting with a man.

Do not expect to close a deal on the first meeting. It is the exception rather than the rule that this will occur. You may occasionally close a deal or get the contract on the first meeting in Germany or Switzerland, because in these countries, executives rely more on written contracts and less on personal trust than elsewhere. But as a result, the terms of the deal and the language of the contract may be even more detailed than your original version.

On the other hand, you must be aware that in some parts of the world, the U.S.-style written contract does not mean the same thing as it does to us. It may not be an acceptable form of doing business at all in some countries. In the United States and a few European countries a contract is considered a binding obligation, but many cultures consider the idea of a written contract insulting. In others a contract is considered a non-binding expression of what both sides hope to achieve. In the Middle East a person's word is even more binding than a written contract. To renege on one's word is unthinkable, and within Arab society deals are made and kept on a handshake. This is the reason for extensive face-to-face meetings. The client wants you to get to know him as much as he wants to get to know you. Mutual trust is the single most important basis for doing business in most parts of the Far East, Middle East and Latin America.

One of the major difficulties Americans have in negotiating overseas comes from the notion that we think we have a commitment when we don't. In Japan, it is considered insulting to say "no" flatly, so "yes" sometimes means "maybe" or even "probably not." Often when a "yes" answer is given, it is not in agreement to the terms offered, but only means that the proposal is understood. When a deal is finally closed between a U.S. and Japanese company, the Japanese themselves often prefer that the contract be written in English, to avoid this kind of ambiguity. They find that English is a better language for expressing the specific terms of a complex deal.

It is hard for some U.S. executives to understand how different the business culture of a foreign country can be. In the Middle East, all services, including the price of a taxi ride, are negotiated beforehand. In China, tips are often given *before* a service is performed to ensure good service. These practices are very different from the accepted manner of doing business in the United States, where we do not negotiate the price beforehand or tip in advance. We assume that for the most part, charges will be fair and within the market rate. In the United States, tips are given as a reward for good service, and withheld as a punishment for poor service.

While most Americans wouldn't think of going on a vacation without at least a sketchy knowledge of the country they're visiting, it rarely occurs to businesspeople to do research on these vital matters of doing business in a different culture.

One of the ways to smooth over less than cordial attitudes is to learn all you can about your client's business culture in whatever amount of time you have. If you are suddenly asked to leave for Colombia, China or Czechoslovakia in a hurry, run to the nearest library or bookstore and read whatever you find about the country—on the plane, if you have to. The more you know about a country, the better you'll be able to negotiate a deal. Of course, most assignments overseas are given in advance, so you will probably have an adequate amount of time to prepare yourself.

Learning about a country's history, politics and social customs will show you how some current practices and attitudes have evolved. If you have the time, a good way to take an up-to-the-minute reading of the climate for women in general is to spend a day watching people go about their business. If you leave your home base on a Friday or Saturday, and recover sufficiently from jet lag by Sunday, become a tourist for a day. Go to a park, museum, square, market or store and watch people interact. Even if women still walk behind a man, it doesn't mean it will be difficult to do business for you, an American woman. But knowing current attitudes can help you to avoid making a major error. Try to know what major political and social trends are affecting the region you will be working in. For instance, throughout the Middle East, there is a resurgence of Islamic fundamentalism that has some effects even in liberal countries like Egypt. In parts of Europe, particularly Germany and some Scandinavian countries, there are some growing anti-American feelings concerning installations of nuclear weapons. In some parts of Latin America, there is resentment about the foreign debt and repayment situation. By understanding the current situations you provide yourself with knowledge that helps you to deal successfully.

The informality that characterizes U.S. business relationships is not shared or appreciated in most foreign cultures. While Americans are very serious about business, our domestic negotiating styles seem breezy and low-key. When doing business in any other part of the world, do not call anyone by their first name unless you are invited to do so. Even in many Western European countries, it is offensive to call someone by his or her first name. For example, people in Germany and France who have worked side by side for years may still call each other Mister or Miss.

In most countries, including Europe and the Middle East, you will be dealing with executives on the upper levels of management. There is less delegation of authority than in the United States and most high-level managers refuse to give up authority to middle managers. In the Far East there is somewhat more group decision making, but those involved are usually on the upper levels of management. In negotiating, you cannot be too formal. Speak softly, clearly and slowly. While many of your contacts will speak English well, they may not be able to understand rapid or colloquial English. More often than not, they will speak British English, which is the same for the most part, but has important differences in vocabulary and usage.

For example, you can cause a lot of confusion in some countries if you try to put off discussion of a difficult issue by saying "Why don't we table that?" In the United Kingdom and in former British colonies, to table an issue doesn't mean to put it off for another time, but to put it on the table for discussion now. If you want to avoid confusion use only standard English and say, "With your permission, gentlemen, let's discuss this issue at our next meeting."

In most cultures, you do not get down to business very quickly. Preliminaries are decidedly formal until a genuine relationship of mutual respect and friendship has developed. In Latin America and the Middle East particularly, you must be prepared to sit down and drink coffee and discuss non-business issues. But even a woman should not inquire about the wife and family of a Middle Eastern client; he would never discuss this at a business meeting. It is acceptable to say, "I hope your family is well," but leave it at that.

In Latin America, you should discuss the cultural heroes, the beauty of the scenery, the rapid growth of the country and its industry or sports. In the Middle East, the rapid growth of technology, the high quality of your lodgings and food and the excellence of the coffee are acceptable topics of discussion.

In Europe, while you may inquire after the family, it is not necessary to prolong small talk to the extent done in Latin America, the Far East or the Middle East. Most Europeans speak English and other languages fairly well (and are continually amazed that most Americans do not speak any language beside English). You will probably be dealing with someone whose business card indicates their professional title (engineer, lawyer, Ph.D., and so on) as Europeans still consider management or administration less prestigious than the professions. In Italy, for example, most educated professionals are called *dottore* or *dottoressa* even if they don't have Ph.D.'s or are not in medicine! Even if you're not sure if someone merits the title *dottore*, use it anyway. Your negotiating partners will be pleased at this flattery.

In the Far East and Southeast Asia, a good way to begin is to compliment people on the truly spectacular growth and development of the country. In Japan, a handshake is acceptable but a slight bow at the waist will be greatly appreciated.

In all countries, if you are offered coffee, tea or a soft drink, accept it whether you want it or not. To refuse is an insult, particularly if the country prides itself on the excellence of their beverage.

Always allow your client to set the pace of the negotiations. Never try to hurry things along. Your knowledge of the host country, your intelligence and sensitivity and the professionalism you bring to the meeting will be your greatest assets.

Women have a tremendous advantage over men in international negotiating. The style of negotiating known as "pull," in which you involve the other person in solving your mutual problem, is a skill many women have mastered. In a decision-making or negotiating situation, many women seek everyone's opinion and try to build consensus. When women do this at business meetings in the United States, male executives present sometimes become impatient and frustrated at this seeming failure to "get to the point." But this is the negotiating style that succeeds in the Far East, Middle East, Latin America and some European countries. Where American men are interested primarily in the outcome of the negotiation, women are interested in the process as well. The pull style of negotiating allows for the expression of feelings in a non-adversarial way. Good negotiators build trust by allowing people to express their needs and feelings. The pull style of negotiating also includes paraphrasing what the other person has said, supporting the other person and exploring the common ground.

Research has shown that the most successful negotiators are those chameleon-like men and women who seem most like their client or customer. The more closely matched the physical, social and personality characteristics of the two negotiators, the more likely that a sale will occur. Women are of course physically different; however, the social and personal characteristics of U.S. women are often a far better fit with men of foreign cultures. Women, with their ability to involve and support, allow others to view themselves favorably. The more a negotiator can make prospective clients view themselves favorably, the more likely it is that they will reach agreement. Women are able to create a comfortable environment for their presentations because they have well-developed social skills. Women are more attentive and patient, compliment others more easily and naturally and make friends more quickly than men.

All negotiations must take place in an atmosphere of trust and sincerity. The more trustworthy and believable the client perceives the negotiator to be, the more likely it is that a deal will be consummated. Women are frequently more open and candid than men. Very little business will take place overseas without trust, patience and understanding. Women's avoidance of risk taking also finds them better prepared for the tasks of international negotiating. Successful women will take the time to learn about the client's needs, interests, preferences and lifestyle without becoming impatient or seeming patronizing.

Many businessmen have failed in their attempts to do business in many parts of the world because they have used the "push" style of negotiating instead of the "pull" style. "Push" includes persuading by using logic, debates, facts and proposals. This style also includes asserting or applying pressure by telling the clients what they want, what's in it for them or what will happen if they don't agree.

Because these (mostly male) executives use styles of negotiating that are so unsuited to countries overseas, they rarely get the chance to make their sales pitch. But even when they are patient enough to have the opportunity to make a presentation, the push style probably wouldn't have succeeded anyway. It is simply out of sync with the tempo of business in many parts of the world. The push style of negotiating overseas leaves little room for uncertainty. The major reason that it doesn't work in a foreign atmosphere is that a decision is always forced by this style. It draws to a yes/no conclusion with little of the ambiguity that is so necessary in dealing successfully overseas.

Another error often made is to try to close the deal at the first meeting. This makes many overseas clients wary, because a trusting relationship has not yet been developed. The traditional U.S. salesman would not want to make more trips, nor would his management want him to. This would be costly and time consuming to their way of thinking. But this short-sightedness is much more costly in the long run. What sales and management need to understand is that to do volume business over the long-term requires an investment of time in the short term.

One of the successful negotiator's biggest tasks is to educate management in the home office about the differences in time required to bring the deal to completion. Few deals are closed on the first meeting anywhere in the world. Repeat visits always have to be scheduled. Even if, in a rare case, a deal is concluded on the first visit, after-sales relationships must be cultivated. When a deal is closed, the successful negotiator does not pack and run. She will invite the client(s) to a dinner where they will celebrate their agreement, for in the successful deal everyone is a winner.

Future meetings in the client's country or in the United States should be suggested and planned for. A great amount of time must be spent, but a business friend made overseas is not just a source of increased or repeat purchase, but can open doors to a vast market.

In a recent study done at a leading business school, 41 men and 23 women were videotaped in a simulated negotiation situation. The findings concluded that when a man visualizes a domestic negotiation situation he sees it as a one-shot deal to win or lose, like a sport or game. A woman sees it as part of a long-term relationship. This shows again that women are better suited for international negotiating than most men.

The interlocking relationships in business overseas are so complex and circuitous that one small successful deal can lead to introductions to previously impenetrable markets. For the same reasons, the loss of a deal due to insensitivity toward one foreign client may seriously hurt your chances of closing a deal with other companies in that country.

Almost all successful international negotiators share the following traits: They ask questions and reveal feelings (without sounding naïve); they use few reasons to back up arguments; they check often to make sure they are understood; they avoid irritating, probing, confrontative statements, counterproposals and defend/attack stances; and they label speech ("If I could make a suggestion . . ."). In many cultures, directness is not appreciated and can be interpreted as abrupt and hostile.

Some of these same characteristics are considered ineffective in business meetings in the United States, but they are precisely the attributes for successful negotiating in most countries overseas. While men in the United States typically grab the floor by interrupting another speaker, women have been conditioned from childhood to believe that it is impolite to interrupt and will wait for a turn to speak. In U.S. business when a woman does speak up, she may undermine her credibility by using tentative phrases such as "I think," by turning statements into questions or by making indirect statements. A woman may say, "Maybe we should send the widget" or "Don't you think we should send them the widget?" instead of "Let's send them the widget." This lack of being presumptuous, while considered a weakness in the United States, is an asset in doing business overseas.

The successful negotiator knows more than the proper style of international business negotiating. She also knows how to use this style in a *cultural* context. Small things like giving sizes, weights and distances in the metric system, and temperatures in the centigrade and not Fahrenheit scale and knowing that the words "billion" and "trillion" refer to different numbers in some countries than they do in the United States are contributions you can make to change the image of the ethnocentric American.

It is important to begin the process of negotiation before you leave the United States, through correspondence, telexes and telephone calls. For Japan and other parts of the Far East, and for the Middle East and Latin America, a better way of beginning a business relationship may be to contact the representative of your client's company if it is large enough to have an office in the United States. For smaller companies, a trade association, social organization, government agency or bank in the United States could be contacted for introductions. Try the Arab-American Chamber of Commerce, Latin American Chamber of Commerce, Japan Trade Center, European-American Bank or the commercial attaché in the country's embassy or consulate. Through these resources you may be able to meet an influential or informative person who can provide introductions for you.

If you have written letters and have not been answered, don't conclude a complete lack of interest. Your reply may not be forthcoming if the client has limited ability in English, needs more time to think about your offer or needs more information about your company. Send another letter with supporting information about you and your company. Do not become impatient or feel insulted if a month elapses before you receive a reply. Continue finding ways to explain your purpose. Show knowledge and understanding of the country's history, culture and business practices (even in a letter!). Make references that show your expertise in your product or business area. If you receive a reply that shows even the slightest interest, make plans for a face-to-face meeting. Again, in most countries business will not progress further until and unless this meeting takes place.

In preparing for your meeting there are certain universal rules to follow: Learn something about the political, historical, cultural and business background of the country. Know the company with which you are dealing (the international edition of Dun & Bradstreet or company tear sheets ordered from D&B are a worthwhile investment). Be able to speak at least a few words of the client's language; if you are reasonably fluent, so much the better. Know your product or service completely and be able to answer all questions concerning what you are selling or negotiating.

Be prepared for a little surprise on your client's part at his first sight of you, even if he already knows you're a woman and is happy to deal with you. Consider your efforts an investment, as the contract or deal you negotiate will take some time but your rewards will be for the long term.

Make sure you bring an adequate supply of business cards. If working in Japan and China, have them printed in Japanese or Chinese on the other side. If you run short of cards you can have them printed on fairly short notice in almost any country. Your business card is even more important overseas than in the United States. It is extremely important in Japan, where there is an etiquette of ways to present and receive cards. In all countries you should stand up when presenting and receiving cards. When you receive a card, read it carefully and either keep it in front of you or put it away. If you put it away make sure you know the person's name so you don't fumble in your pocket to look at the card. In all countries offer a firm handshake; in Japan, add a slight bow.

In almost every overseas business encounter, you shouldn't expect to conclude substantive matters during the first meeting. This meeting is a getting-to-know-you exercise. The further away you get from Western Europe, the more your client will want to know about you and your company. Allow some time for your client to get used to you, the executive woman. It is not likely that he (or they) will have done a great deal of business with American women previously, so this is your opportunity to show your professionalism, ability, sophistication, calm and wit—in short, all the things in which women excel.

If you have been made to wait for your appointment for what seems like an inordinate amount of time, do not feel insulted. Understand that others, especially Arabs or Latin Americans, do not experience time in the same way that people in the United States do. Don't assume you are being discriminated against because you are a woman. Above all, do not refer to the amount of time you have been waiting, as it will make it obvious that you are irritated or insulted and give your client an upper hand in negotiations. Time has a lesser priority in certain countries throughout the world. Similarly, in Japan, meetings are usually held on time, but the negotiations can be subject to endless delays due to the Japanese style of decision making.

Your initial meeting should revolve around mutual acquaintances, discussions about each other's country (here it is always useful to have read a book by an esteemed author, seen a victory by the country's soccer team, heard some music of the country or have some similar experience to discuss) and suggestions for future meetings. This might be the time to invite your client to drinks or dinner with his associates. While your client will feel he is in control of the meeting, it is you who will in fact be controlling the situation. If your client does not feel threatened or rushed, as he might if he were negotiating with a U.S. businessman, your dealings will be easier.

If your first meeting is held at lunch or dinner, keep in mind that in most countries it is not polite to discuss business while eating. In the Middle East and India, do not use your left hand while eating unless you are taken to a Western-style restaurant and presented with a knife and fork. You will probably not be served alcohol in Moslem countries; if it doesn't appear, don't ask for it.

In most (non-Moslem) societies a toast is always appropriate, preferably with the local wine or spirit. Watch out for other cultural norms with which you may not be familiar. For example, in Japan it is considered rude to blow your nose loudly in public.

Another cultural factor to be aware of is the concept of space. Americans conduct business at a distance of about two to three feet; but overseas, particularly in Latin America, the Middle East and India, conversations are held at very close proximity. Recognizing this is particularly important for women. If your client stands three inches away from you, this does not mean that he is making sexual overtures.

If your client is standing very close, it is most important to avoid taking a step back to increase the distance between you and him. This is perceived in Latin America and the Middle East as the proof of the American coldness that they have heard about. In Great Britain, Germany, Switzerland and parts of Scandinavia, cultural norms are somewhat similar to those in the United States, but in all other places, know your client's differences and be sensitive to them.

All your preliminary discussions are a part of the negotiating process. In many places, if the preliminaries are not to the client's liking, and he feels that a real relationship is not beginning, there will be no further negotiations. During these preliminaries it is a good idea to avoid discussing religion and politics.

In the Middle East, everything is dictated by religion and a negotiation may be stopped to allow for the prayers that are called for five times every day. Since most of Latin America is moving toward democracy, the subject of politics is not quite as volatile as it once was. Acknowledge the new leaders and progress, but avoid opinions on ideology.

There are a number of European countries where the young population is increasingly anti-American. Germany, for instance, has a highly militant group that resents the United States for its "nuclear proliferation." Other countries such as France, Greece, Spain and Italy have moved toward socialist policy and are at times critical of the United States. Avoid falling into traps of agreeing (no matter what your feelings) or disagreeing. Try skillfully to change the subject.

Before you sit down at the bargaining table, be sure to define your own goals. Try to understand beforehand what the client's objectives are. Since price and quality are not the only important things in a deal overseas, learn what "alternate currencies" can be offered to sweeten a deal. These may be in the form of a longer warranty, an option added at no extra charge, a relative considered for employment, a stock option or any perk that may increase the attractiveness of the deal.

When you finally progress to the negotiating stage of your relationship, be sure you are aware of the business characteristics of that country.

GIFT GIVING IN DIFFERENT CULTURES

Small gifts are appropriate in any business negotiation anywhere in the world. Items such as pens, pen sets, key rings, small tools, cups, flashlights and the like, engraved with your company's logo, are not only appreciated but virtually essential. These gifts are more advertisements and mementoes than gifts and should be considered as part of the advertising budget.

In many countries where you need to develop a long-term personal relationship in order to do business, larger gifts may be appropriate. In Latin America, a good bottle of Scotch and U.S. cigarettes (especially Marlboro) are much appreciated. Recently Scotch and U.S. cigarettes also seem to be the gift of choice for clients in the People's Republic of China.

While alcohol is prohibited in most of the Moslem Middle East, cigarettes are not, and your Arab and Israeli clients alike appreciate U.S. brands. In most European countries, entertainment in the form of dinner at a good restaurant or tickets to the ballet, opera or a concert are preferred gifts. Of course, if you know your client's family quite well, it is also appropriate to give a gift to children in the form of a U.S.-made toy or game.

In Japan, gift giving is an important part of the culture. One of the gift-giving seasons begins July 15 and lasts for a month. This is timed to the summer salary bonus that is standard in Japan. If you are negotiating during this period, you should present a gift to your client and be prepared to receive gifts in return. Glassware, food, alcohol and designer items are highly desired.

Of course, if you are in the midst of negotiating in a country where Christmas is celebrated, gifts are in order.

Be aware, however, that there are certain gifts that may be totally inappropriate in some parts of the world. Cheese is not eaten in China, where it is considered to be spoiled milk, and your client would be upset to receive it. Clocks are objectionable in China because the word for clock is similar to a word associated with a death ritual. Linen handkerchiefs are associated with sadness in Brazil, and knives may indicate cutting off a relationship in many parts of Latin America.

In most of Europe and in Japan, U.S. jazz records are extremely desirable gifts. In France, West Germany and Scandinavia especially, a large number of people are jazz enthusiasts and consider U.S. jazz to be the only acceptable form of that music. In Japan, U.S. jazz and rock and roll records are sought after.

Large gifts, on the other hand, are not usually appropriate to give or to accept. An expensive item given or accepted may be considered a bribe and often puts you in a compromising situation, ethically or legally. It is best to know the laws and attitudes concerning bribery, giving gifts of high value and making large donations to charities in the country you negotiate in. Giving gifts of high value is generally condemned in the United States, but in many countries, gift giving on a somewhat higher price level is acceptable or even the rule.

While giving a gift as the price for awarding of a contract or closing of a deal may not be illegal, U.S. business executives may have some ethical reservations. If a donation to a legitimate local charity greatly increases your chances of closing a deal, it should be considered as part of the cost of doing business.

How can you determine when giving or accepting a gift becomes a bribe? Intent is one way to determine the difference. If you or your client perceive that a gift is simply an excuse to improperly influence the other, then it is obviously a bribe. Secrecy is another indicator of an inappropriate inducement. In many Arab countries, gift giving is done in public, so that the giver's generosity will earn him respect. If a large gift is clandestinely offered or received, you may be running into trouble. For example, a U.S. executive was traveling in Saudi Arabia and received a paper sack while boarding the plane back to the United States. The negotiations were not yet complete and the Saudi was still seeking concessions from the U.S. company. Opening the bag on the plane, expecting to find a snack, the executive discovered a half dozen expensive watches. Recognizing this as an attempt at bribery, the executive returned the watches.

Gift giving, however, is a private affair in many Asian countries and a privately given gift would not necessarily be considered bribery.

Large gifts may often involve a breach of law or ethics. While a large gift to the owner of a privately owned business overseas, or a donation to his favorite charity, is probably not illegal, a large gift to a purchasing agent, for the purpose of influencing his judgment on behalf of his company, is unethical, and, in some places, illegal. (For example, many U.S. states and some foreign countries have laws prohibiting commercial bribery. Even if not illegal, it is often bad business ethics.)

Bribery of foreign government officials by U.S. business may be in direct violation of the U.S. Foreign Corrupt Practices Act of 1977. While bribery is accepted and acceptable in some countries, especially of low-level, poorly paid functionaries, high-level bribery is not. For example, if you want your shipment of perishables to be inspected before they rot, it is wise in many countries to attach a $5 or $10 bill to the invoice or bill of lading. This is considered greasing the wheels of commerce and is regularly accepted. To influence a choice between equals (your company versus another company closing a deal) giving a U.S.-made small appliance or other moderately priced gift is also usually acceptable. However, giving a large gift to secure a deal to which your company is not entitled is improper. For example, a large sum of money given to an official for exclusive purchase of your disinfecting chemicals, whether they are competitive or not, would be considered an illegal bribe.

In some places, most notably Mexico and Italy, commercial and individual bribery is a way of life. Be certain to research what is and isn't acceptable and be careful of running afoul of the local laws as well as of U.S. law. In these cases, especially, it is helpful to have a local contact advise you of standard practice. If that is impossible, do as much research as you can on the local customs and practices before you begin your negotiations.

A WORD ABOUT THE FOREIGN CORRUPT PRACTICES ACT

In 1977, upset about political scandals caused in some foreign countries where top government officials were found to have accepted bribes from U.S.-based multinational corporations, Congress unanimously passed the Foreign Corrupt Practices Act (FCPA).

The major provision of the FCPA prohibits any U.S. based company from "corruptly" giving or offering money or "anything of value" to a foreign political official, "for the purpose of obtaining or retaining business." The requirement that the payment be "corrupt" excludes "grease payments" such as small tips to low level government clerks for routine approval of export documents. To be illegal under the FCPA, the payment must be to a foreign government official or to an official of a foreign political party. But in many parts of the world, where industries are state-run or where governmental "consultants" act as go-betweens on business deals, the application of the FCPA to ordinary business deals can be quite broad. Bribes are illegal even if paid indirectly, such as when a U.S. company reimburses the "expenses" of a foreign subsidiary or a local distributor, knowing that some of the money will be used for bribes. The FCPA carries severe criminal penalties, including large fines (up to $1 million on corporations) and jail sentences of up to five years.

Other provisions of the FCPA require U.S. companies to adopt accounting practices that will enable top management to be aware of any bribery being carried on by low-level sales people or by foreign subsidiaries.

Many provisions of the FCPA are quite technical, such as rules specifying what percentage of stock a U.S. parent must own in a foreign subsidiary before it will be held responsible for the subsidiary's actions. Other terms in the law are vague, such as the prohibition on payments made "corruptly." Here, as with any situation on the border between innocent gift giving and illegal bribery, your wisest course is to check with the legal department at the home office before making a payment that might later be questioned.

The Reagan Administration has not made the FCPA a top enforcement priority, and there are frequent proposals to modify the law, especially by those who claim it is losing sales for U.S. business in many parts of the world where bribery is common and companies based in other countries are not limited by the FCPA. But the law remains on the books, and caution is still advisable.

5

Doing Business in the World Marketplace: Asia and the Middle East

JAPAN

Despite the complaints by many U.S. companies about Japanese protectionism, you *can* do business with Japan, if you have the patience and knowhow. In Japan you will probably have to start your negotiations with a middle manager. At this level you should be as detached and technically accurate as possible. You will then speak with the general manager or director who is a step higher in rank. He will want to hear about your firm's background and reliability. He will also want to know something about you and your experience. While in recent years U.S. women have been doing business with Japan, the Japanese are still not comfortable with women in positions of power. (Japan is, after all, still one of the most macho cultures in the world.)

At all meetings, speaking even a few words of Japanese is greatly appreciated. With the introduction of each person, be sure to present your business card so that it is facing the client and not upside down.

Whatever your proposal is, make sure that you can support it with facts. Many Japanese executives are so much better informed about the West than we are about Japan that you must be sure of your facts. When business talks are in the initial stages in Japan, your Japanese client will be sizing you up. It is not until your negotiation progresses to very serious consideration (if it does) that your Japanese counterpart will reveal what he really feels about your proposition.

Always speak clearly but softly, and use only standard English. Unless your client speaks fluent English or you speak fluent Japanese, use an interpreter who has been recommended. The added advantage of interpreters is that they can modify your direct talk to conform with the Japanese way of thinking. In Japanese communication depends on who is talking to whom. There are many levels of honorifics (deferential titles) and many levels of politeness. Always remember that in Japan, it is important to "sell" yourself before you can sell your product or service.

The progress of negotiating the deal may be frustrating, because it seems much slower than in countries like the United States. Don't let your exasperation show. Try to keep a slight smile on your face or to show no emotion at all.

Your client may appear to be avoiding giving a direct answer to your offers. Often, Japanese have difficulty in saying "no" to any part of your proposal, even if they do not agree at all. This results from the wish of the Japanese to present at least an appearance of harmony. Remember that *hai*, the Japanese word for "yes," doesn't always mean agreement, it often means only "yes, I understand what you are saying." A direct "no" is considered rude. The Japanese way is to talk around a subject for so long and in so many ways that everyone understands the other's point of view. No one loses face because no one has to back down.

If you're confused as to whether your clients are really in agreement, ask directly but respectfully for their opinion, explaining that you would be grateful to have opinions expressed to avoid any misunderstandings later.

Sometimes during a meeting in Japan, your client will interrupt the negotiation to call for tea. This utilizes a style of negotiating known as disengaging. When tension is high, or the negotiator wants time to think, disengaging provides temporary relief. You may also want to use the tactic of disengaging at some point in the negotiating process (not only in Japan, but anywhere in the world) by asking for a glass of water to give yourself an opportunity to recoup or to refocus your proposal.

Sometimes during an impasse in the discussion, your Japanese client will remain silent. At other times, your client may not even respond to a question, not feeling compelled to say anything. Do not become uneasy or make clarifying statements. This is where many U.S. businessmen voluntarily give in on a disputed point or say something they shouldn't just to get the conversation started. These few minutes of silence are only another form of disengaging, not an example of manipulative or shrewd behavior on your client's part. Silence is a way of stepping back and pondering the question.

The group decision-making process is still common in Japan. This is one of the reasons why negotiating is so time consuming. The final decision is based on a consensus of many individuals. It may take a long time and you will have to participate in endless meetings. However, when the decision is finally made, implementation of the program quickly follows.

At the same time that the "Japanese management style" is becoming popular in the United States, the Japanese are beginning to admire the style of management they think of as "American." A recent *Fortune* article reported that a leading Japanese newspaper published a list of the best-run companies in Japan. The first and second places went to companies that were run autocratically or as a "one-man show." These aggressively run companies could be prototypes of Japanese competitors in a quickly changing world.

Do not forget Japan's endless fascination with the United States. They are just as mystified by and interested in us as we are in them. There is constant imitation of each other's customs and innovations. This is fertile ground for profitable business dealings.

CHINA

Negotiating a deal in the People's Republic of China is one of the biggest business challenges you may ever face. This market, of more than one billion people, has just recently been opened to foreign trade. In some ways, China is totally unique, unlike any business culture you will ever encounter. However, certain features of the Chinese business culture are very similar to those of Japan, including lengthy negotiations, the concept of face and the importance of business cards. In fact you will find these similarities in other parts of Asia: in Taiwan and Korea, particularly, and in Hong Kong, Singapore, Malaysia, Thailand and Indonesia to varying degrees.

The Chinese have very strong incentives to attract foreign ventures. One reason is that they have over 400,000 old factories to renovate. The two dozen foreign investment laws passed in recent years to ensure the legal protection of these ventures indicates the Chinese commitment to foreign trade. Special economic zones have been created to absorb foreign technology and learn Western techniques. Inside these zones a free market system is being established. Although the Chinese press may deny it, the zones are enclaves of capitalism within China.

China has also begun a major effort to expand its trade with the United States. China imported over $5 billion worth of goods from the United States in 1984 and much more is anticipated every year.

You and your group (the Chinese prefer to deal with a group rather than a single negotiator) will probably be greeted at the airport by a welcoming party and sent off to your hotel. When you meet your Chinese client, offer your business cards, which should be printed in Chinese on the reverse side. Here, as in any culture that respects age, you should express the hope that your client (who is likely to be much older than you) is in good health). When beginning your meetings, be prepared for lengthy negotiations. Negotiating with Chinese ministries or corporations over the simplest contracts may take months, with many visits needed and delays occurring frequently. The Chinese bureaucracy still has a built-in inertia at the middle management level. Your constant, patient attention is required to ensure progress on a deal.

The more advance information you can give your Chinese client about what you hope to accomplish in and for China, the likelier you are to be pleased at the results. The Chinese do not like surprises in their business dealings with Americans; they prefer to know exactly what issues will be raised so they can have responses planned ahead of time. Early information allows them to line up the most appropriate participants on their side, so that you will be more likely to talk to the proper counterpart.

When your Chinese clients enter a room, they generally do so in protocol order, with the highest ranking person coming in first. The exception is the interpreter, who is next to the delegation leader, in order to provide him with a voice. The Chinese assume that the first member of your negotiating team is also the head of the group. You can avoid the confusion of having a recording secretary taken for the CEO by observing the Chinese protocols. Your client may occasionally have a woman in the negotiating team, as one of the principles of the Chinese communist system is to promote sexual equality. After you are introduced, and cards are exchanged, be sure to address your client correctly. The Chinese put their surname first and given name last; the given name is rarely used in conversation.

Meetings in China always begin on time, but small talk and politenesses are exchanged before any serious discussion. As in Japan, it is considered impolite to get down to business immediately. Discussions of the weather, your stay in China and the other cities in China you have visited are good ways to break the ice. Internal politics or foreign policies are *not* suitable subjects for discussion. You shouldn't mention Taiwan even if you have recently been there on business or pleasure. Don't bring up the growth that China has experienced, as your client is well aware of the many problems still facing the country.

When you finally get the signal to begin discussing business, you should pause frequently so that the interpreter can digest and translate your remarks. There is a very wide cultural gulf to be bridged because China has been isolated for so long. As in Japan, if your client seems to sidestep direct questions, it is either because he or she doesn't know the answer or because the answer is no, which it is considered impolite to utter. If you get an indication that your client needs to check on something before giving an answer, ask him to designate the contact person with whom you may follow up later. This will help speed the negotiating process.

Be aware that your client may try to pressure you to make concessions. He may try to convince you that other companies are interested in the same contract. If other firms are in the running, your client may exaggerate the concessions that those companies have been willing to make. Don't be pressured into giving the store away. Try to negotiate with alternate currencies such as warranties, perks, and so on. As a courtesy to your client, have copies of your proposals translated into Chinese, so that lower-ranking officials can study them.

Either you or your client can end a meeting. The ranking group member can comment on how much of the client's time he or she has already taken up and politely request that another meeting be scheduled.

Even more so than in Japan, the negotiating process is an art that requires great skill and patience. As there is virtually no private sector in China, everything is controlled by the government, and you cannot do business in China without the support of an official body. Just getting the okay to do business in China can take time, and much more time will be taken up by the actual negotiating process when you do get the go-ahead. But negotiating in China may be well worth your patience. While waiting three years for the first order to go through or to secure the joint venture may seem inordinate, the Chinese market is well worth the trouble because brand loyalty is very strong in China.

The concept of trust is an important part of deciding whom to award the contract. Before a contract is awarded or a deal made, the Chinese have to come to respect you as an individual. The process they use to determine your sincerity often includes a banquet. While it is important not to make serious social mistakes at these ceremonies, minor gaffes are not critical. You can politely refuse the sea slugs without losing the deal. Your attitude is what counts. Your usual sensitivity, caution and careful observation of others' behavior will ensure your success. Toasting your host with alcohol or other beverage is customary. Conversation need not be complicated; in fact, you are best off sticking to discussion of the excellent food, or of the Chinese language, climate and geography. Be careful about putting anyone on the spot by asking questions. Embarrassments are considered a serious breach of etiquette. Do not attempt to become personally friendly with anyone in your client's group, as China does not encourage individual friendships between foreigners and Chinese citizens. "Friendship" refers to cooperation and good working relationships between your company and the Chinese group. Toast the friendship of your company with China, enjoy the food and, as always, be patient.

Patience paid off for Barbara R. Pick, Executive Vice President of General Robotics Corporation, a Hartford, Wisconsin manufacturer of computer parts and systems. After 20 weeks in China and three different trips, Pick in 1983 secured two major contracts for her company totaling $8 million—more than doubling company sales.

TAIWAN

The Far East is the fastest-growing industrial area in the world, and U.S. business travelers are spending a tremendous amount of time there. Negotiations may be long and tedious, but the results can be spectacular.

Taiwan is a fast-growing, aggressive economy located only 90 miles off the Chinese mainland. Taiwan is light years away from China in its capitalist economy, and has industrialized so rapidly that its infrastructure hasn't caught up. The Taiwanese do a great deal of business with the United States, and Taiwan is an excellent market, particularly for U.S. services. The Taiwanese like and admire Americans. The people are ethnically Chinese, but may have been educated in the United States, making Taiwan an interesting amalgam of old-fashioned Chinese sensibilities and modern Western ideas. A very important thing to remember when doing business in Taiwan is not to mention Mainland China or local politics.

Despite the vast political and economic differences, many of the same customs are observed in Taiwan as in China, although within a more relaxed atmosphere. Once again, be sure to have your business cards printed in Chinese on the reverse side, and prepare for your negotiation in a manner similar to that in China. The banquet is an important part of a business relationship. Observe the same protocols as in China. In addition, you should bring small gifts to your client. Negotiations cannot be rushed, but there is a great desire on the part of young Taiwanese to continue the country's development at a rapid pace. You may find things moving more quickly than you anticipate, but should never be the one to hurry things along.

KOREA

Korea is, in its rapid development, somewhat similar to Taiwan, and in some ways has also been compared favorably to Japan in its aggressive growth. However, it is wise not to make any comparisons between Korea and Japan, as Koreans are sensitive about the dominance of Japanese business in the region. Koreans are outgoing and somewhat less formal than the Japanese or Chinese. However, the same concepts of "face" are very important to Koreans. Age, position in society or business and education are highly respected in Korea.

Because of the sensitivity of the division of the country into communist North Korea and capitalist South Korea, it is unwise to discuss anything having to do with local or international politics. The best topic of discussion includes the exponential growth rate achieved by Korea over the last 20 years.

The majority of the population shares only three family names: Kim, Park and Lee. It will be easier for you to use titles such as Manager Lee and Director Kim to avoid confusion among similarly named members of the delegation.

Even though English is widely spoken in Korea, it is a good idea to use an interpreter, especially if you are negotiating a very sensitive or expensive deal.

Koreans can sometimes seem very direct in their questions, but it is not a sign of rudeness, it is simply a sign of interest. Conversely, formal manners and behavior are very important in negotiating until a relationship of trust has been established.

SINGAPORE

Singapore is a physically attractive, rapidly developing island nation made up of 75 percent ethnic Chinese, and minorities of Malays, Indians and Eurasians. Many of the young wealthy Singaporeans study in European and American universities and have rapidly accelerated the pace of doing business. The country is clean, and laws are strictly enforced. Women are often highly educated and work in the arts and professions.

Be punctual at your meetings, as being late is considered rude. Good opening topics of conversation are places you have visited and the beauty of Singapore. Avoid any religious or political comments. Singapore is a very modern Asian country and quite Western-looking. English is spoken widely and most people are bilingual.

Do not try to get to know your Singaporean client in a hurry. Wait until you have met the client a few times before inviting him or her to dinner. Do not invite public-sector or government officials to dinner as they are not permitted to accept. Interestingly, once you have established a relationship with your client, you can even discuss business over a formal dinner!

HONG KONG

Hong Kong is a British Colony with a 98 percent Chinese population. English is the official language and business is conducted in English. Hong Kong is a strange blend of the Asian and European with a totally international demeanor. Hong Kong is a center for international banking and finance. However, with growth have come all the irritants of modern society. Hong Kong has one of the more corrupt business systems in the world. In the last ten years or so, this corruption has come under closer scrutiny of the government, but has proven hard to eradicate.

When doing business in Hong Kong, be careful and get to know your client as well as possible. Here again the concept of "face" must be respected. The obligatory banquet is an integral part of the negotiations.

Hong Kong's attitude toward women in business is not totally liberated yet. But the vast amount of U.S. business done with Hong Kong is bringing women on negotiating teams, and the close business relationship with mainland China's more egalitarian society has also had a positive effect on the climate for women.

The negotiating process is slow in Hong Kong. As in any country with a history of corruption, caution is necessary. If you are going to Hong Kong to establish a link with Mainland China, be sure that your contact is legitimate.

You should also be aware of the practice of *fung shui*, a popular form of occultism. The best times and circumstances for beginning negotiations may be determined by a *fung shui* expert. If your client proposes such a ritual, do not ridicule it; respect it and then get on with business.

SOUTHEAST ASIA

Thailand and Indonesia are two developing nations in Southeast Asia. The Moslem religion predominates in Indonesia, and the Buddhist in Thailand. Your sensitivity to the customs and laws involved is an absolute requirement to doing business in these countries. Both countries are quite poor and the pace of negotiations is extremely frustrating and slow. While you may encounter some difficulty as a foreign woman in a Moslem society, there are no major legal restrictions against women doing business in Indonesia. In fact, in both countries, there are some women in senior positions, particularly in privately owned businesses.

Negotiating in Malaysia may pose some problems for women. Approximately 45 percent of the population is Moslem, with Chinese and Indian minorities. However, the Chinese dominate the business community and you would be most likely dealing with them. Avoid any discussion of religion, as it is a very sensitive issue. Even politics can be discussed, but better yet would be conversations about family, sports or travel. Comments on the success of the client are always appreciated. Carefully avoid comparisons between the West and Malaysia. Again, the concept of "face" must be respected. However, Malaysians are not generally as diplomatic in their dealings as other Southeast Asians.

Your client will be polite and attentive but occasionally suspicious. He will ask you many questions and answer as few questions as he can. Entertainment is an important part of business in Malaysia and you should invite your client to lunch or dinner to follow up on your meeting. Invite all persons involved in the negotiations to join the dinner.

In your negotiations do act humbly and be aware of the Malaysian sensibilities. They are shrewd businessmen and may know a good deal more than they let on.

AUSTRALIA

Australia is a very different type of market in this region. A cross between the United States, the United Kingdom, and Canada, it is not exactly like any of these. Australians are unique, resourceful, friendly and energetic and dislike being told how to do things. In your negotiations, be honest and forthcoming, as Australians regard extreme formality as insincere and artificial. Be careful to avoid comparisons between Australia and the

United States or the United Kingdom. For all their geographical isolation, this Western nation is technologically progressive and very sophisticated.

INDIA

India is an immense and diverse country of over 750 million people. The large majority (80 percent) of Indians are Hindus, but there are significant numbers of Moslems and Sikhs. There are 14 languages spoken in addition to English. To be on the safe side, when meeting with your Indian client, offer a *namaste* instead of a handshake: Place both hands together as in the position for a prayer, and make a slight bow. If you are sure that your client is very Westernized, offer your hand. It is generally not a good idea to discuss the weather in India as it is almost always hot and somewhat uncomfortable.

Part of the legacy that years of British rule left in India is a multi-layered bureaucracy. Your negotiations may have to go through several levels of management before any progress is made. Be patient. This huge democracy has a promising market. Be cautious, however. Everyone in India (or so it seems) wants to do business with the United States. Research your client thoroughly before beginning labyrinthine meetings.

THE MIDDLE EAST

The Middle East is by far the most difficult area for U.S. businesswomen. There are a few places, like Saudi Arabia, that make it extremely difficult for women to obtain business visas. Nevertheless, there are a number of countries, despite the increasing Arabization of the Middle East, where women can work quite comfortably.

The 20 or so nations of the Arab world contain almost 200 million people. Western business executives are traveling to the Middle East in increasing numbers. The wealth of this region and its emergence as the world's major oil producer has made it enormously important to the U.S. and to every country dependent on imported oil.

As a result of the U.S. support of Israel, there is long-standing antagonism toward us in the Arab world. There is an effort in some Arab countries to boycott private companies doing business in Israel. Before any attempt to do business in the Arab world is undertaken, be sure to check the minutest regulations of the country far in advance of any planned visits.

As in Asian cultures, the concept of "face" is extremely important in the Arab world. Arabs are very sensitive to small slights and embarrassments. Avoid any situations that make your client look bad. This sensitivity is related to religion, rank, nationality and class. You should carefully research the country in which you will do business to learn the many nationalities and minorities both within the country and out, and what their current alliances and hostilities are. Intra-Arab fighting has been virulent in the past few years, with more than a few countries continually at war with each other.

Although the Arab world is varied, there are some generalizations that hold for the entire area. The most important factor to consider is the religion, Islam, which dominates life in the Middle East. Many of the restrictions on women derive from the emphasis on traditional values and behavior. Moslems believe that open social relations between the sexes result in the breakdown of family life.

The concept of the family network, quite unknown in the West, can almost be compared to our social welfare system. Nepotism here (as in Latin America) is not a negative concept, it is expected and congratulated. These kinship ties operate at all levels of society and business.

In the Arab world, there is a rigid concept of what work is dignified and allowed. Saudis and some other Arabs will not do any manual labor. They will hire Sudanese or Yemenis to do the dirty work. People are expected to know their place and few try to change their lot. This corresponds roughly to the Latin American sense of place and fatalism, and the belief in God's will.

As in Asian culture, there is great respect for age. Advanced years mean wisdom and command respect. Age takes precedence even over rank. Also, the outright "no" is never given whether in business or social situations. You should avoid the absolute negative in your negotiations. Do not confuse a genuine "maybe" with the "maybe" that really means the unspeakable "no." If you have been avoided or turned aside a number of times, this means the "maybe" is really "no."

Concepts of time and space in the Middle East are similar to those in Latin America, and "tomorrow" isn't always meant literally. Don't be put off by broken appointments. Continue making new appointments and don't show your irritation.

People often sit or stand very close to each other in Arab business negotiations. Part of this has to do with the practice of having at least three "meetings" held concurrently. In order to capture each other's attention, Arabs literally must speak into each other's ears. You probably will not have the problem of uncomfortable closeness. A woman doing business here is so unusual, given the negative Arab attitude toward women, that they will probably stand a good distance away, if they will do business with you at all.

Most Arabs will do business with a woman, but only if they know who she is and trust her. While a woman will never be fully accepted in the Arab social world, there is no reason why she can't develop a relationship of trust with her client. There is no doubt that it will take longer to establish this relation than perhaps in any other region but it can be done with patience, respect for Moslem tradition and a genuine desire to become friends. If your client wants your product or service, and you are professional, he will accept you.

Among the Arab countries, Egypt is a relatively comfortable place for women to do business. Cairo and Alexandria are sophisticated and cosmopolitan cities. Egyptians are friendly and liberal by Arab standards. There is no segregation of the sexes and it is legal to drink alcohol in Egypt. Most of your clients will speak English quite well. The capital, Cairo, is large and crowded with almost ten million people.

You will be at a distinct advantage if you invite your client to a European-style restaurant along with a few of his associates and their wives. Women are very much a part of social and business life in Egypt.

In your negotiations, take the time to know your client. While things will not progress as quickly as in Western countries or in Israel, Egyptians are quite Westernized and are comfortable dealing with business executives from the United States and Europe.

Jordan is also a somewhat liberal Arab country with women in public life. Always accept coffee offered by your client at meetings. There will probably be some surprise at your being a woman, but you will not have any major problem doing business.

You can easily obtain a visa for both Egypt and Jordan. All business travelers need a supporting letter from their company explaining the nature of business and confirming their financial responsibility. All Arab countries (except Egypt since 1982) make it difficult or impossible for a businessperson to enter the country if his or her passport shows evidence of a visit to Israel.

Aside from Egypt and Jordan, you should observe strict Moslem protocols in doing business in the Middle East, both in the more liberal Arab countries (Bahrain, Kuwait and the United Arab Emirates) as well as in the more traditional ones. In Saudi Arabia or other very traditional countries, you will probably not be allowed to meet your client in the office, and your meetings might take place in a private home. Moreover, you will have to be sponsored, probably by an embassy, a Saudi family, a corporation or by your husband or father.

In any case, be punctual even if you have to wait. As soon as you enter the client's office (or the client meets you at the home) present your two-sided business card, Arabic side up. Make small talk and avoid discussion of any other countries in the region. Arab disunity and intra-Arab hostility are widespread. Always accept and drink (with your *right* hand) the hot tea or coffee offered. It is a good idea to drink more than one cup, if possible. If you don't want any more, shake the empty cup when returning it. This signifies your refusal.

After pleasantries have been exchanged and your client indicates that business may begin, start your presentation. Prepare it in small segments as there will often be interruptions. People may wander in and out of your meeting unannounced. Try not to lose concentration. This is not rudeness, just a different way of doing business. Don't become exasperated or feel insulted. Serial (one after another) meetings are not the rule in the Arab world; rather, several meetings may take place virtually simultaneously.

Your meeting may also be interrupted at one of five prayer times, which occur at dawn, noon, midafternoon, early evening and late evening. The faithful will stop discussions and kneel to pray. Be careful not to walk on a prayer mat, don't stare and never interrupt. These prayers last for only a few minutes at most. You should simply sit quietly and wait.

During your meeting, be careful not to hand your client any papers with your left hand. If you are left-handed take extra caution. The left hand is considered unclean, and using it is an extreme insult.

Take care to avoid any business trips to the region during the month of Ramadan, when Moslems are forbidden to eat, smoke or drink from dawn to dusk! The month of Ramadan does not correspond to any particular month of the Western calendar, so be careful to check before your trip.

After you have made your presentation and drunk your final coffee, it is time to take the initiative in leaving. If your client wants you to remain or continue, he will urge you to do so; if he does not urge you to remain, this indicates he has heard all of your proposal he intends to hear.

Arab businessmen put religion and family before business. Deadlines do not have the same impact on Arabs that they do on Westerners. Time is not considered controllable by human beings and God's will cannot be changed. All of this makes for a very unusual way for U.S. executives to conduct business. Since almost everything is deemed more important than negotiating, meetings may be put off or ended abruptly.

Try to avoid direct eye contact with Arabs, especially in Saudi Arabia. Most people in the United States believe that eye contact is a prerequisite for an honest relationship but many Arabs are adept at reading the response of your pupils, which dilate when you are really interested in something and contract when you don't like something.

While most Arabs speak English, it is a good idea to know a few words of Arabic and to be certain to find out in advance if you'll need an interpreter. Rank is important when dealing with Arabs, particularly the Saudis. They want to deal with someone who has decision-making authority. If they think you are not of sufficiently high rank, they may take it as an insult, since they interpret this to mean that your company does not consider the Saudi or the project important enough to send out a person of rank. This can easily become a reason for them to back out of a project or to refuse to deal with you.

In most cases you want to know the reasons for changes in attitude or interest in your project. Stay alert to your client's attitudes and try to turn things around if you feel your client is losing interest. Women have an advantage here as their sensitivity to mood changes is frequently greater than men's.

As among the Chinese, Saudis will always let you know that you are competing against other companies. They often will know prices and terms that other companies can offer even though they are dealing only with your company. This is a way for your client to show that he is knowledgeable and not gullible.

Alternate currencies such as training in the United States for your client or his son or managers, an invitation to the United States for business or vacation or any personal assistance for your client and his family will make a great difference in the outcome of your negotiations. By offering to help your client's family you have gotten to the center of his life. This is the real focus of a Saudi's (and most Arabs') life. This will endear you to him and could possibly be the determining factor in achieving a successful outcome.

One place in the region where you can do business without restrictions placed upon women is Israel. While Israeli society is aggressive and male dominated, women can negotiate in Western style. Israel has a very strong relationship with the United States and actively seeks to do business with U.S. firms. Israel's fast-growing, innovative technological base makes it an attractive country for investment, countertrade, licensing and franchising arrangements, and for all forms of joint ventures.

When you sit down at the negotiating table in Israel, be prepared for aggressive bargaining. Israelis are demanding and the business pace is very fast by Middle Eastern standards. While macho attitudes always prevail, you can, by taking the time to learn a little about Israel's recent history, strike a deal in a fairly short time. Almost all Israelis speak English, as it is commonly taught in schools. Be firm, polite and friendly.

6

Doing Business in the World Marketplace: Latin America and Europe

LATIN AMERICA

Latin Amrica is the name most commonly used to indicate Mexico, the Spanish-speaking Caribbean and Central and South America. Although generally lumped together, these places are vastly different. While all the countries in Latin America speak Spanish except for Brazil, the people, their culture and sensibility diverge widely. The Dominican Republic is as different from Argentina as Greece is from Sweden.

There are 400 million people in Latin America, half of whom are under 20 years old. Even though the debt situations of Mexico, Brazil and Argentina now seem overwhelming, these countries are very fertile future markets for U.S. business. In the last few years, democracy in varying degrees has returned to all the countries of South America except Chile.

As in the Far East and Southeast Asia, some general observations hold true for most Latin Americans. Most countries have small elite groups that control a good portion of the country's wealth. These are the landowners and big business owners. There is an emerging middle class, particularly in the newly industrialized countries such as Brazil and Mexico. The largest group is the poor, who are the workers, poor farmers and the urban underemployed.

While the overwhelming majority (about 98 percent) of Latin Americans are nominally Catholic, the degree of actual observance varies from place to place. Many countries have strongly anticlerical attitudes. Other countries, especially Brazil, combine Catholicism with African-based spirit religions. There is a fairly strong belief in fatalism, the idea that life follows a preordained course in which human fate is determined by the will of God. For the U.S. business executive with a "where there is a will, there is a way" attitude, this attitude of fatalism can severely disrupt any planning and scheduling and cause tremendous frustration.

The concepts of personalism and dignity strongly affect the workings in Latin American organizations. Personalism, or the recognition of each person as an individual, prevents many Latins from blending into the anonymous conformity required for smooth organizational functioning. Dignity often prevents Latins from doing whatever is necessary to get the job done if this involves dirtying their hands. Latin America is still very stratified socially, and one is either born "high" or "low." While all of this is beginning to change, there is still the combination of fatalism and "place" (the level at which you are born) that prevents many in Latin America from striving to get ahead and move up the corporate, educational or professional ladder.

Decision making in Latin America is effected by this class system as well. The person in authority has the power to make decisions without consulting others. Any questioning of that authority would imply lack of confidence in his judgment. A worker or lower authority would never question the decision of the person in charge.

The concept of machismo is not limited to Latin America, but certainly is at its most extreme there. Latin males respond to aggression, heroism and charisma much more than to logic, persuasion and consensus. Machismo is often most pervasive at the lower levels of the social scale where prowess is a substitute for real power. In business negotiations you will be dealing mostly with upper-level, educated, fairly powerful men who are less likely to display overt macho tendencies.

The negotiating situation in Latin America provides women with the opportunity of using another "pull" style known as attracting. In "attracting" you produce desired behavior by providing a positive vision of the future, and exploring the common ground. You present the vision of what could be "if only Tadpole Tractors were used" in the construction of new homes for workers. The implication is that your product will lead to comfort, prosperity, jobs and an improved standard of living.

When you begin meeting with Latin Americans, you and your client will spend a good deal of time in the process of getting to know each other. As in the Far East and the Arab world, serious business is never conducted until and unless a relationship of trust is established. Greet your client effusively, comment on his healthful appearance, ask after his family and always mention the rapid development of his country's economy. Make sure you know the names of some local heroes and patriots, sports stars, artists, musicians and writers. Get to know your client. Show genuine interest and respect and, above all, have patience.

In Latin America, formalities reign. Always address clients as señor (senhor in Brazil), señora (senhora) or señorita (senhorita), or as Mr., Mrs. and Miss, and their surname. Use of a first name is insulting unless you have been asked to use it.

Don't discuss politics unless you are asked, but make sure you know about the particular country's political leaders and situation before you begin your meetings.

Do not be surprised if your meetings do not begin on time. In Latin America time is not perceived in the same way as in the United States. You should arrive for an appointment at the agreed-upon time, but be patient if you have to wait. Your client's lateness or keeping you waiting is not a sign of rudeness or disrespect to you. It is often simply another manifestation of the system of kinship ties, under which a manager or employer's first obligation is to his family and friends. A request from or discussion with a friend or family member will always take precedence over the business at hand.

If coffee is offered at the beginning of your negotiations, always accept it. You do not have to drink more than a bit, but to refuse the offer is insulting, especially in those countries where coffee was the main cash crop at one time or other. (Besides, you may find, as I did, that you like the coffee in Latin America better than anywhere else in the world.) If your meeting begins with everyone standing around for a few minutes conversing informally, be very conscious not to step back when a Latin American moves closer to you than you'd like. Their idea of space is different from that in the United States. Conversational distance is usually comfortable to us at anywhere from two to three feet, but for Latin Americans this distance is no further than 12–18 inches. Your client is not trying to make sexual advances when he steps closer, and you must avoid the impulse to move away. There is a widespread belief in all parts of Latin America that people from the United States are cold. Much of this stems from our concept of space, and from the way the typical U.S. nuclear family has diminished over the past 25 years. Latins perceive us as lacking in friendship and kinship ties so vital to the Latin personality.

Some of this belief has also come from the insensitivity of U.S. businessmen's dealings with Latin America. The jovial, backslapping wheeler-dealer didn't try to pursue a long-term relationship, but took the money and ran, leaving bad feelings behind. In many Latin American countries, most notably Mexico, there is a lingering distrust of U.S. businessmen. Mexican businessmen sometimes attempt to get even by canceling meetings, making frustrating overtures, dragging out negotiations and generally exhausting his U.S. counterpart. Mexicans will then attempt to take advantage of that exhaustion when the businessman loses patience and gives away more things in a negotiation than he should.

Don't try to rush negotiations, and don't give up if meetings are canceled. Continue pursuing your client. If after you meet a few times and all your attempts to begin serious negotiations are thwarted, you may be tempted to give up. Don't! Let a few days pass and begin again. You are only being tested for your sincerity. If you give up easily you won't be regarded as serious. Swallow your anger, forget your pride and thus you will prove your sincerity to your client. Once this obstacle has been overcome your negotiations will be easier. It takes a long time to be trusted and regarded as a friend in Latin America, but once it happens, it is for the long term and can be a vital business advantage.

The businesswoman who succeeds in negotiating has learned that Latin America is not one country. Although there are exceptions and some countries fall into more than one category, the 18 nations of Spanish- and Portuguese-speaking Latin America in which you are most likely to do business fall into five general groupings. Each of these five markets is different from the others; they have little in common except for language.

Caribbean Latin America

Caribbean Latin America includes Puerto Rico, the Dominican Republic, Panama, Honduras, Caracas and coastal Venezuela, the coastal cities of Colombia such as Barranquilla and Cali and the Spanish-speaking population of Miami and Tampa, Florida. This group is characterized by a tropical climate, a fairly large black or Creole poor population and a small upper class, which controls most of industry and politics. People are warm, open and friendly, and are often admiring of the United States. Most industry is labor intensive and low tech.

While you will encounter a good deal of machismo in these places, as in many less developed countries, it will not seriously hinder your progress. Your negotiations are apt to be slow, interrupted, repetitive and occasionally neglected. Adapt a nonpressuring but formal stance, retain your sense of humor and have patience.

Mexico

Mexico is in a category by itself because of its strategic importance to U.S. business and the difficulty of negotiating there. Mexicans have never forgotten about the U.S. annexation of the Southwest. This fact, combined with extreme nationalism, fatalism, the current debt and inflation situation and, paradoxically, a pervasive belief in the superiority of U.S. goods, makes for a love-hate relationship between the Mexican people and U.S. visitors. Mexicans are very proud of the progress they have made independent of U.S. influence. It is a good idea to learn about the economic accomplishments and to praise them effusively.

Do not expect your appointments in Mexico to begin on time. Even Mexican businessmen joke about specifying *hora Americana,* distinguished from Mexican time, when they want to indicate punctuality. Remember that Mexicans are North Americans, so be sensitive when discussing geographic regions. Never call people from the United States "Americans."

Mexico's proximity to the United States hasn't benefited Mexican women much yet in the development of careerism. It will take some work for your Mexican client to get used to you and accept you. Be cordial but firm. Mexico is probably as difficult a place for U.S. businessmen to negotiate in as women, because of the fear and hostility created by images of big brother from the North coming to pillage again.

It is very helpful to speak at least a few words of Spanish, and if at all possible a few of the Mexican idioms. While many Mexicans speak English very well, you may encounter some executives who staunchly refuse to use it in the negotiating process. Be certain to find out in advance if you may speak English at your meetings. It may be useful to have an interpreter along in any case. In the course of contract negotiations in Mexico remember that Mexicans treat the contract as a work of art and an expression of the ideal. A contract expresses a goal to be strived for, not a binding obligation expected to apply consistently in the real world.

You will probably encounter more macho attitudes in Mexico than in any other part of Latin America except for the Caribbean. While this may be off-putting, remember that Mexico is a huge and growing market of over 75 million people right on the southern border of the United States. The proximity, size and demand of the Mexican market make it worth your while in spite of all the canceled, forgotten or ignored meetings and other frustrations and delays.

Brazil

Brazil, the third category, is somewhat different from the rest of Latin America as it is the only Portuguese-speaking country on the continent. Brazilians are sometimes called "Luso-Americans" (derived from Lusitania, the ancient name for Portugal). It is a huge country with 130 million people. The first civilian presidential election in 21 years was held in January 1985, putting a democratic government in office. Inflation is high and Brazil owes nearly 100 billion dollars in external debt. Nevertheless, Brazil is an excellent place to do business for the long term. Half of the population is under 20 years old and there is tremendous pent-up demand. U.S. goods are highly valued and sought after. The Brazilians admire the United States and its economic strength. There is a positive attitude on the part of the Brazilians toward doing business with us.

It is important to remember when exchanging business cards that, in Brazil, Paulo Lopes Almeida is called Senhor Almeida. Brazil differs from Spanish-speaking Latin America in this regard; in Mexico (and other Spanish-speaking countries) José García Rodríguez is called Señor García, never Señor Rodríguez.

Brazilians have a great zest for life, and nowhere is this more evident than in Rio de Janeiro. Your meetings in Rio will be relatively informal in nature with an unhurried pace. The South, especially São Paulo, is far more European and business-like in style.

When you sit down at the negotiating table you will be offered coffee. Never refuse it, as coffee provided the cash to build the great cities of Brazil. You don't have to drink it all, a sip will do so long as it is followed by a comment on how delicious it is. Milk will not be served along with it but sugar and a glass of cold water will. It is powerful but this is what coffee is all about!

Knowing a handful of words of Portuguese earns you respect automatically, because any number of U.S. businessmen before you have made the inexcusable error of using Spanish at their meetings. Many Brazilians in executive positions speak English well, but you should always be sure to ask in advance if you may speak English as in a few cases you may need an interpreter. Whatever you do, don't speak Spanish. Brazilians all understand Spanish, but are proud of being different from their Spanish-speaking neighbors and regard the use of Spanish as insulting.

Begin your discussions with comments on the rapid growth of the country's cities, the beauty of its beaches, or other aspects related to Brazilian culture.

There is a great internal competition between the cities of Rio and São (pronounced something like the English word "sound" without the "d") Paulo. Rio is said to be the heart of Brazil and São Paulo the pocketbook. Differences between Cariocas (those who live in Rio) and Paulistas (residents of São Paulo) are much like those between (Los) Angelinos and New Yorkers. A popular Brazilian newspaper cartoon shows a bikinied man and woman on a beach in Rio watching a man in a suit carrying a briefcase hurrying across the beach. The caption says, "That's our new neighbor who recently moved here from São Paulo."

São Paulo, in the south of Brazil, is a great industrial center, looking more like Chicago than anywhere else. Business there is formal, intense and punctual. The pace is fast and relatively straightforward. As opposed to tropical Rio, São Paulo has a more temperate climate, and its inhabitants have a tremendous zest for doing business. While you still have to observe rituals such as coffee drinking and introductory discussions, you will probably be able to conclude negotiations faster here than in Rio or other Brazilian cities such as Brasilia (the capital) or Belo Horizonte.

Brazil's ethnic makeup is fascinating. The population is composed of largely European stock in the southern states of São Paulo and Rio Grande do Sul, blacks in the Northeast, and Indians in the still partly unexplored Northwest. You will encounter every color and combination.

You will encounter much less machismo in Brazil than in Mexico. Women are often in the professions such as medicine, education and journalism, and occasionally are small business owners. While few Brazilian women are in managerial or executive capacities, you as a U.S. woman will find little resistance to doing business in Brazil.

European Latin America

European Latin America includes Argentina, Costa Rica (in Central America), Chile, Colombia, Uruguay, the city of Lima in Peru, and the aforementioned southern part of Brazil. Aside from Argentina, you will find negotiating in these countries and cities the most familiar and the most like Western Europe in all of Latin America.

Argentina and Uruguay particularly identify very strongly with European traditions and ways of life. While both countries have had a long history of right wing leaders, they now have democratically elected presidents who seem to be improving the overall economy. At the turn of the century, Argentina was the economic equal of Canada, but has steadily declined.

Argentina, with a long history of fascism, political instability, foreign debt and inflation, is a difficult country to work in. Argentines are very proud, sometimes to the point of arrogance; according to the *New York Times* (April 25, 1982), they consider "Brazilians monkeys and Americans (U.S.) uncultured." They are educated, sophisticated and believe that the capital Buenos Aires is a spiritual outpost of Paris. In many ways they're right. Porteños (residents of Buenos Aires) are chauvinistic, secretive and difficult to warm up to. The capital is lovely and if you squint, the boulevards seem to resemble those of Paris. The pinstriped men, the activity of the *bolsa* (stock exchange) and the general demeanor do in fact recall Paris. You can break down their resistance to you personally, and in doing business, by acknowledging this resemblance and commenting favorably on their sophistication, charm and European graciousness.

In Bogotá, Colombia, Lima, Peru and in Chile and Costa Rica, you will be able to conduct your negotiations in a manner similar to most of Western Europe. These people are gracious, formal and receptive to U.S. executives. Chile, the only country in Latin America still under a powerful dictatorship, has declined sharply in the past 10 or 12 years. Chilean women are educated and, at least before the recent political crackdown, were quite liberated and outspoken.

Your negotiations in "European Latin America" will be fairly punctual, formal and reserved. Coffee will be served and you should always accept it. Observe general guidelines for doing business in Europe.

Indian Latin America

Indian Latin America includes Bolivia, Paraguay and Ecuador, in South America, and Guatemala and El Salvador in Central America.

While Spanish is spoken in the large cities, the rural areas speak Indian dialects almost exclusively. Even in the cities, negotiations will be slow and drawn out. People are generally courteous, friendly and steeped in Indian tradition. As a result you must be patient in negotiating and continually reiterate important details. It will take quite some time to complete your dealings but perseverance pays off.

EUROPE

You will find that Europe is the most familiar climate in which to negotiate, but don't be lulled into thinking that Europe is an easy place to do business or that the people are the same everywhere. If your travel experiences in Europe have been limited to vacationing in a city or resort, be prepared for very different attitudes on the part of the Europeans in business situations.

Many Europeans speak English in addition to their own language. It is not unusual for a European to speak two or three other languages—well. The countries of Europe are mostly quite small geographically, and most border on several others. This proximity provides for a good deal of cultural intermingling and intra-European business. However, each country is very different from the other in history, politics and economics and in the national personality and attitude. There are often vast differences even within one country. Northern Italy is much more like Switzerland in many ways than it is like Southern Italy.

There are, however, some generalities found throughout Europe. Despite some recent change, the old social structure still dominates throughout Western Europe. Society is stratified by family tradition, and most working-class people do not become educated past high school. University education is still primarily for the upper classes. Most Europeans still disdain the concept of business; it is far more acceptable to become educated as a professional. Doctors, lawyers, engineers and professors are more respected than business executives. You will, however, find many people in business who were trained in the professions. The business school curriculum as we know it in the United States is rare and few Europeans want the title Master of Business Administration. Business executives may use their previous professional titles such as Doctor or Lawyer.

Business in Europe is not nearly the all-consuming passion it is in the United States. While in many countries, notably Germany and Austria, work is taken very seriously, even in those countries, business is not the primary focus of life. People work hard and put in long hours but are somewhat less driven than Americans. In most of Europe, the tradition of gathering in cafés, traveling, reading or relaxing is as important as working hard. Almost everyone in Europe gets a month's vacation annually. In the United States it may take years to earn that much vacation time.

As in Asia, Europeans highly prize experienced people rather than young go-getters. A newly minted M.B.A. from a top school without any experience can earn fantastic sums of money in the United States, but Europeans are not very impressed with this credential. Europeans are fairly risk-averse and most people prefer a modest but secure position rather than a chancy, exciting opportunity.

European thrift and economy are remarkable, particularly in Germany, Switzerland and Belgium. People there will repair rather than throw away, save rather than spend and in general make do. These are characteristics of 2,000-year-old cultures, as opposed to the 200-year-old culture of the United States. Consequently, change is somewhat slower in Europe. While there are many women who work, there are fewer women who are career professionals than in the United States. Female executives on the middle and upper management levels are few, but their numbers are beginning to grow. Recently, a number of lawsuits by European women seeking equal pay for equal jobs have begun to make headlines.

It is evident that many U.S. techniques are being adopted in European business practice. While the fast-track pressured atmosphere has not been imported, certain U.S. marketing and advertising concepts have been successfully transplanted to Europe.

Northern Europe

The Scandinavian countries of Denmark, Norway, Sweden and Finland are small, modern and fairly easy for the American business executive to deal in. You can probably call your younger client by his or her first name after the first few meetings. People are for the most part well educated, fairly liberal and friendly.

Your presentations will be heard and given sincere consideration. Be certain of all your facts and quotes. Most Scandinavians speak English very well and enjoy using it. Be punctual for your appointments and avoid becoming involved in discussions of U.S. politics.

There are many people in the United States who have the misguided perception that Scandinavian society is totally liberated and pro-feminist. This is mostly myth; Scandinavian culture is quite traditional, especially in regard to female careerism.

Among these countries, you will find the people in Denmark the most friendly and the most comfortable doing business with women. The Swedes are somewhat more formal and reserved; the Norwegians are also fairly formal, and are more provincial. You will find a few female executives everywhere, but probably more in Finland than in the other Scandinavian countries.

Elsewhere in Europe, you will find that the business culture in the Netherlands (Holland) is somewhat similar to that in Scandinavia. This is also true, to a lesser degree, in Belgium. Punctuality, a certain degree of formality tempered with warmth and a desire for privacy characterize these countries.

The countries of Germany, Austria and Switzerland are highly formal in business matters. First-naming is almost unheard of, even among colleagues who have worked together for years. There is more informality among the younger people, but you should always use Mr., Ms. or Doctor to be safe. Punctuality is extremely important in these countries, as is observance of formal social etiquette.

Always begin your meeting with some non-business conversation. Discussing some aspect of the country that you enjoy is a good way to open. Let your client set the pace of the negotiations. Younger Swiss, Austrians and Germans are somewhat more open and informal, but it's best for you to be conservative in your approach. Moving rapidly into business discussions could set up a somewhat defensive reaction, particularly if you're dealing with the older generation. Your knowledge of your product and of contracts will earn the respect of your client. Once you can win your client's confidence, it will be yours forever.

In contrast to the Japanese, many Northern Europeans, particularly Germans, have a low tolerance for ambiguity. Be sure to spell everything out in careful detail. A German contract specifies details that contracts in the United States might leave to standard trade practice.

French businessmen are also somewhat formal and conservative although not nearly as much as they were 20 years ago. Except for younger or international executives they do not usually use first names. Using Madam and Monsieur without the surname is your best bet. The French often react negatively to new ideas at first, but can be won over after considerable discussion. Rational arguments supported with facts and figures are the most successful tactics. Allow your client sufficient time to examine, question and talk about all aspects of the deal. Your presentation should be understated and unpressured for the best results.

Southern Europe

Italy is a study in contrasts. Negotiating in Rome, or anywhere to the south, is vastly different from doing business in the northern cities of Milan or Turin. Northern Italy is more like Switzerland in concepts of time and space while southern Italy is more languid, informal and macho.

When beginning your meeting it is not necessary to spend much time making conversation. It is perfectly acceptable to shake hands and begin discussing business after a brief preliminary chat. Your client will expect you to be very well briefed on your products or services, their applications and what they are being used for in other countries. Most Italian executives will be quite courteous to you and will try to avoid giving a definite no answer even if they are not interested in your offer.

Italians are fairly formal in their business dealings and first names are not generally used. A common honorific is *dottore* and most executives will respond positively even if they are not Ph.D.s.

When dealing with Milanese, you will find a stronger business orientation and a more positive attitude toward female executives. Romans often take U.S. businesswomen less seriously. Of course, it is difficult to inquire from what part of Italy your client comes, so a formal approach is usually the best.

Business should not be discussed at dinner or at an informal gathering. Italians are very family oriented and inquiries about family are appreciated. Discussions about sports, particularly soccer, and international affairs are popular.

Doing business in Spain sometimes feels like negotiating in an advanced Latin American nation. While executives in Madrid and Barcelona may have had some contact with businesswomen, they may not be as used to dealing with them as their counterparts in Italy. It is only 10 years or so that the repressive Franco era officially ended with the dictator's death. There has been tremendous change in that short amount of time. In 1975, it was just barely acceptable, and certainly unusual, for a U.S. businesswoman to lunch alone at a fashionable executive's restaurant. Now it is more commonplace to see business-suited women in formerly male preserves in Madrid and Barcelona.

When you begin your meeting, always shake hands effusively and pass around your card to everyone.

In the past few years, formality has given over to first-naming after initial introductions. Business in Spain is often conducted over drinks and sometimes over dinner. Always return the invitation if you are asked to dinner. Spaniards are friendly and warm people and, like Italians, are very involved with their families. Another favorite subject is bullfighting. Spaniards take this sport very seriously; even if it is offensive to you, do not comment upon it negatively.

Since Spain is still somewhat traditional with regard to attitudes toward Spanish women, it is wise not to discuss the incidence of careerism among Spanish women with your client.

It is easier for a woman to do business in Portugal than in Spain. The culture is less formal and somewhat less male dominated. Women in Portugal hold more management positions than women in Spain or Great Britain.

Great Britain

Don't be misled into thinking that because people in the United States and United Kingdom both speak English there will be easy understanding and similarities in the manner of doing business. Winston Churchill's comment about "two countries separated by a common language" is nowhere more applicable than in business.

Not only can language be misunderstood, but gestures often mean different things in the United Kingdom than in the United States. Because the English and American languages and social customs are often similar, your caution may be reduced. But a simple hand gesture that in the United States is used on the floor of the commodities exchange to mean buy or sell, has an obscene connotation in urban London.

The differences, of course, go much deeper than the obvious ones of language and gesture. The British way of thinking is often radically different from that in the United States. As a result of centuries of doing things in a traditional way, the British have a slight resistance to rapid change, and do not move with the same urgency that Americans do. Not even Londoners share the sense of competitiveness that characterizes business in all large (and many smaller) cities of the United States.

The British prefer to keep their private lives out of the business arena. They will not conduct business 24 hours a day as is often the case in the United States. The entire pace of business is slower and less frenetic than in the United States.

When negotiating with your British counterparts, whether in England, Scotland, Wales or Ireland, be certain to say "British" and never "English." Even when you are in England, many of your clients may be Irish, Scots and so on and you can avoid uncomfortable political errors if you speak only of "the British."

British business appointments are very punctual, but not always formal. The younger generation of business executives is far more informal than the older one, but exceptions abound. Here, as in almost every country in the world, don't rush. You will probably be offered tea, which you can accept or decline without insulting your client. The British are very fond of Americans for the most part and often enjoy discussing the United States vis-à-vis the United Kingdom.

The British sense of humor is extremely different from that of the United States. It is often bawdy, always dry. Most jokes attempted by British often fail to elicit responses from Americans, and vice versa. Avoid humor unless you have a deep sense of British wit.

Your presentation will always be given a thorough hearing. Be careful to use only standard English, avoiding trendy phrases and words. Your British clients may misunderstand the latest New York or Los Angeles expressions.

There are regrettably few women in management in the United Kingdom, although there are a fair number of women in the professions. There is, however, little resistance to dealing with a woman executive from the United States, in part because England has a woman prime minister and the British are aware of the incidence of business and professional women in the United States. Combined with respect for U.S. business acumen, this business climate makes negotiating with the British a rewarding experience.

NEGOTIATING WITH AMERICANS:
A LIGHT-HEARTED GUIDE FOR THE UNINITIATED

While I was writing the last few chapters, I had a funny thought: if a woman from overseas were writing about doing business in the United States, what would we sound like to a foreign audience?

If you're in a hurry to get to your next meeting, you can skip the rest of this chapter. But if you can still enjoy a small laugh at our own expense, read on.

The United States is vast in size and influence. The 230 million people who live between two coasts are 3,000 miles apart geographically, and at least that far apart culturally. A New Yorker flying to Los Angeles for a business meeting will often be surprised to find that it is being held in a hot tub. It takes almost as long to fly from New York to California as it does to London. On arrival, the culture shock is likely to be extreme in both cases.

The United States is a young, dynamic and sometimes naïvely unsophisticated country. For a person coming from overseas, negotiating with Americans can be a traumatic but ultimately rewarding experience. To begin with, if Americans allow the time for meaningless pleasantries, they will often reveal personal details or ask embarrassing questions. Introductions are fairly standard, complete with business card. Many executives from overseas are astounded to see so many women on the managerial level. These women are usually introduced as Ms. Jane Smith or Ms. Sally Jones and then, as do U.S. businessmen, ask to be called by their first names. The pace of negotiations doesn't slacken, and soon the overseas client is asked to produce a price list, often before having finished the first cup of coffee. This is just as well, considering what American coffee tastes like.

Try to match the U.S. executives' pace to some extent, but if that is too exhausting, slow them down by asking them to talk about their favorite subject: themselves. Americans, particularly New Yorkers, will freely talk about their education since primary school, how much rent they pay, politics, prices, families, almost anything. Don't discuss religion as the United States is a very diverse society. Stick to a less controversial subject like nuclear disarmament or sex.

Women are in direct competition with men in the United States, and will often match male behavior. Lately, women have begun to interrupt men, correct them when they are wrong (and sometimes when they aren't) and, in general, stand up for themselves. The peculiar habit of women wearing the same navy blue or gray suit and bow tie is beginning to fade as women become more secure in their own professional identity, but you will still find some women executives dressed as clones of their male colleagues. Do not compliment them on their shade of lipstick.

It is fortunate that most foreign executives speak English because few Americans speak anything but. Regional accents and rapid speech make most Americans hard to understand, so ask them to slow down politely and they will—for at least a minute. Americans are almost always prompt for a meeting, so don't be surprised if they fuss and fume when you are only 30 minutes late. They have no way of knowing that back home you would be ridiculed for arriving so early. Be patient. When your meeting begins and everyone shakes hands, be certain to step back a bit. Physical proximity makes Americans nervous and they avoid touching if possible. You need only observe a crowded subway car during rush hour to understand how New Yorkers can be packed like sardines and still avoid touching.

Most Americans are fanatics about personal hygiene. Remember, this is the country that invented deodorant sprays for parts of the body you didn't even know existed. But paradoxically, in many U.S. cities garbage proliferates and people allow their dogs to "foul the footpath."

You may or may not be offered coffee. And you do not need to accept, particularly if you dislike the brown liquid served in foam cups that impart a chemical taste, served with powdered "creme" and sugar that never saw a cow or cane.

It is usually not necessary to allot more than an hour or two to conduct any business, as Americans are very bottom-line oriented. They want to see a price list, or the final offer, fast. They don't rely on personal relationships in business because they are very mobile. Americans don't need to form a relationship with you because they will probably be at another company the next time you call. They depend on contracts rather than relationships of trust. So, grin, bear it, make the sale or deal, go out for a leisurely 20-minute lunch with your client and move on to your next appointment.

7

Breaking Down Barriers: Five Stories

Women are receiving assignments overseas in increasing numbers. However, the reception they get upon arrival varies greatly. Even within the same country, a woman may be accepted easily in one city and treated rudely in another. Often, the farther away from Europe you go, the more difficult it becomes to be accepted. Nonetheless, women have and will continue to conduct business successfully, even in remote and unusual places throughout the world.

Barbara Stewart, an investment manager, has traveled to the Middle East a number of times. She has successfully conducted business in Saudi Arabia, Tunisia, Jordan, Iraq and Egypt. While doing business is vastly different in Egypt than it is in Saudi Arabia, Ms. Stewart feels that "if they want your product and you are professional they will accept you anywhere in the Middle East."

She thinks her success is based on understanding how the society works and knowing what to expect. Barbara explained that while men have easier entree into Saudi Arabia, they must have contacts already established, just as a woman would. No one can expect to get to Saudi Arabia and then make phone calls to set up appointments. This must all be prearranged, and channels of communication must be established in advance. Ms. Stewart doesn't mind the restrictions placed on women in Saudi Arabia. Yet, even as a Westerner, the official and informal rules that restrict the freedom of Arab women were applied to her. (This is true however, primarily in Saudi Arabia and only rarely in other Arab countries.)

She didn't mind wearing long sleeves and a long skirt. "It's not terribly different from my New York uniform of dark blue suit, long sleeve blouse and low heel pumps," she adds.

Barbara met a number of Saudi women who are doing business. However, women in Saudi Arabia may do business only with other women. Many of these businesses are fairly large in size. Women in Saudi Arabia have their own bank as well. Ms. Stewart notes that a good deal of money is controlled by women in Saudi Arabia as in other countries in the Middle East. Saudi women, however, are extremely restricted professionally. They are only allowed into a handful of professions, including teaching at a segregated school and writing for the women's section of a newspaper. Many of these young women seem to be defensive about the restrictions placed on them. Barbara Stewart believes that many of these young women have been influenced by the recent resurgence of Islamic fundamentalism.

In Egypt, women work side by side with men and rarely wear the veil. Women socialize with men, and many are involved in the arts. Ms. Stewart enjoyed the relaxed tolerance in Egypt. While the country is basically conservative, in Cairo and Alexandria there are no restrictions on business interactions with women.

In Amman, Jordan, things are somewhat similar. Again, Barbara could hardly wear jogging shorts, but she was free to move about anywhere on her own, even to have dinner alone at a restaurant. Ms. Stewart traveled to the Middle East while she was single. In some places she invented a husband, in order to forestall any questions about her personal life from both men and women. However, she was often questioned about her husband's feelings about her travels. Now married, she explains truthfully that he doesn't mind since she is only away for a few weeks at a time. Barbara says that after the first few times, it's like traveling for business in any other place in the world: exhilarating, but exhausting.

Eugenia Thackeray, a senior-level U.S. government public relations officer, traveled widely in the Far East and was posted in Indonesia for three years. She felt that it took her a year to acclimate to her surroundings and to think less like an American. Ms. Thackeray said that one of the biggest differences between Asia and the West is the importance of tranquility. In most Western societies noise, motion and agitation abound, both publicly and privately. For Asians, however, nothing is more desired than tranquility and quiet. A low, calm soft voice will get people's attention much more quickly than abrasive shouting.

Genie said that the Far East differs from the United States particularly in the level of formality. Asians are rarely casual the way people are in the West. It is unthinkable to sit in a chair or sofa sprawled out American style.

Throughout Asia, personal contacts count for everything. Ms. Thackeray explained that it took a while for her to be accepted by the Indonesians; her Indonesian counterparts who worked at the U.S. installation were the contacts that helped her break the barriers. They introduced her to key people and gave her entree to Indonesian society. She spent a lot of time chatting about the loveliness of Indonesia before she was able to begin doing business. Ms. Thackeray learned that she could not usually come directly to the point. If time was pressing and she felt the need to speed up the pace of the discussion, she would say, "May I be terribly American?"

As she was accepted into Indonesian society she was invited to weddings and parties, and learned to converse indirectly with everyone she met. She discussed trips, families and food, but always in an impersonal manner. Genie had to revise her thinking in order to speak about personal things impersonally. She invited all she met to visit the United States and never, ever said anything critical about Indonesia. She pointed out that in Asia you must never lose face or embarrass other people by asking questions they don't want to answer.

In negotiating a price for a seminar, Ms. Thackeray discovered that in Indonesia prices are never firm. In the United States for the most part our price is that on the price list. Most U.S.-to-U.S. business is done based on that price and only occasionally is the price bargained down. In Indonesia, as in many other parts of the world, any price is considered negotiable.

Bribes occasionally are part of the Asian social structure as well. Genie Thackeray had to suppress her distaste and accept totally changed values. One highly prized way to thank someone for a favor done is to give a small wrapped gift, with a "Made in the U.S." label clearly in sight. Despite this unpleasant practice, Ms. Thackeray came to enjoy the different customs of Indonesia and found it somewhat difficult to readjust to the "boorish" attitude of U.S. business.

Noelle Johnson had no prior experience in dealing with the Japanese until she was given a gift by a friend who had spent some time in Japan. Ms. Johnson, an artist, was particularly impressed with the gift, which used a proprietary process that would transfer designs onto ceramic. She thought that the kits would make excellent gifts for do-it-yourselfers who were interested in making pottery. Noelle did some research and learned the name of the manufacturer. She wrote him a letter explaining her interest in importing and setting up channels of distribution for the product. Ms. Johnson received a letter saying that the manufacturer, Mr. Ishikawa, was seeking a distributor network in the United States. She began a six-month period of letter writing and telephoning. Fortunately, Mr. Ishikawa was fairly fluent in English. While he seemed surprised to hear that "Noelle Johnson" was a woman, he was still receptive to her. She spoke very softly and made oblique suggestions and references to what she wanted without asking for anything. She allowed Mr. Ishikawa to come to the conclusion that she might be the best person to represent his product in the United States. Noelle expressed such genuine interest in the product that Mr. Ishikawa began to trust her. When she suggested that she come to Japan to meet the inventor of the process, he was completely won over.

Mr. Ishikawa was enthusiastic about her forthcoming trip. He promised to make introductions for her, teach her more about the pottery and ceramic business and in general show her a little bit about how business is conducted in Japan. She spent the next month reading every book about Japan she could get her hands on. She learned bowing protocol, eating habits and as much Japanese culture as possible. She also learned a few phrases in Japanese, a skill that would ease the awkwardness of many situations.

Mr. Ishikawa was true to his word and taught her the ceramic pottery process in a few weeks. He introduced her to the elderly inventor of the design transfer device. During this time Ms. Johnson did not even mention the possibility of representing the process in the United States. She simply learned all she was taught, made suggestions and was thoroughly appreciative. Mr. Ishikawa and the inventor were thrilled with her professional ability and involvement. She even made suggestions about names for the kit that would be marketable in the United States.

She went back to the United States and spoke to Mr. Ishikawa every two weeks. After six months, Noelle felt the need for more training in the process, and at the urging of Mr. Ishikawa went back to Japan. Mr. Ishikawa told her that, unknown to her, he already had a distributor for his company in the United States. She didn't act shocked but told Mr. Ishikawa she could help train the representative in the process. Mr. Ishikawa thought it would be an excellent idea. Noelle went back to New York and met with the distributor who told her he wanted Mr. Ishikawa's other product lines but didn't want this product. She telexed Japan, and said, "Let me represent your excellent product, since the distributor can't handle it." Mr. Ishikawa gave her a year. She asked politely for a contract and he explained that it is unnecessary in Japan. Noelle explained that in the U.S. market it was absolutely necessary that she have written proof that she was the rep, and Mr. Ishikawa agreed.

Early the next year she took the product to a trade show in which 600 companies participated. Interest was high, but she learned that the packaging and instructions had to be changed for the U.S. market. She asked Mr. Ishikawa for more time and he said she could have two years.

After a few months a major company became interested in the product. Noelle got a contract on a commission deal. She was now the official manufacturer's U.S. representative for "Floramika." Her perseverance, belief in the product and respect for the Japanese way of doing business enabled Noelle Johnson to succeed.

Pat Winters, 24 years old, was told by her boss-to-be during her interviews for a sales position that would possibly include overseas travel, that she would have to work extra hard to be taken seriously because she was young and attractive. She swallowed her anger and took the job. She has traveled widely throughout Europe and has had few problems being taken seriously by her overseas clients. The ambiguity of her name suggested to her European clients (who had only corresponded with her) that she might be male. Her clients were quite surprised to meet her at first, but her knowledge of the country, the culture and the products she was selling quickly became apparent.

During her recent trip to the United Kingdom, Norway, France, West Germany and Italy, her clients were impressed at the extent of her product knowledge. She firmly believes it is this understanding of what she sells, her belief in those products and her enthusiasm for them that makes the age/sex issue less of a barrier.

My experience as a management consultant and as marketing manager for a major trading company centers mainly around Latin America and, to a lesser degree, Europe and the Far East. Prior nonbusiness experience in Latin America and a good command of the Spanish language gave me tremendous insight into a somewhat difficult-to-penetrate business climate. As recently as 1980, when I attended an industrial fair in Bogota, Colombia, I was one of the few professional women present. Of course, there were the ubiquitous glamorous models draped over the stands and equipment, but otherwise there were no women attendees or exhibitors. While trade fairs, even in the United States, seem to bring out the worst in attendees (who are usually men far from home), this fair was made less than pleasant for me because of the unwarranted (and unwanted) attention I received. At meetings, things were somewhat easier, and as the carnival atmosphere of the trade show began to fade, it became easier to be accepted as a professional. It was obvious that the Colombians and other Latin Americans at the show were not used to seeing, much less dealing with, U.S. businesswomen. During the course of the next few years a fair number of U.S. women began traveling to Latin America to do business, and it became easier to be accepted.

Before the debt crisis exploded in the early part of 1982, I had been contracted to do a cost reduction and marketing feasibility study for a large corporation in Mexico City. This was during the time that the Mexican government and corporations were borrowing cash and spending it freely. Many companies were engaged in building conglomerates by all forms of merger and acquisition. In both Mexico City and Monterrey, M.B.A.s from the United States were being courted like royalty. It became part of the corporate growth imperative to have M.B.A. consultants as part of the team. Most people thought that the oil boom and business expansion were permanent features of the Mexican economy. Traditional Mexican resentment toward the United States began to diminish as prosperity seemed near. Nevertheless, Mexican managers were not used to having U.S. women map out acquisition strategies, marketing plans or cost reduction programs. I was treated politely by lower management, but certainly not welcomed. After the first few days of going over the objectives with the English-speaking senior manager, I began to wonder why lower management seemed resistant to my overtures. While I knew that many of the men spoke English, I used my carefully practiced Spanish with them. My recommendations and plans were to be written in English and then translated into Spanish. When I used English with the men, few of them responded. I began to feel frustrated and afraid that I couldn't get enough cooperation to complete my work successfully. One Friday, a group of managers and administrative assistants (one female) were talking about their plans for the weekend. One of the men said in very rapid and slangy Mexican Spanish, "Let's get the hell out of here and have a big blowout tonight." Without thinking I asked if I could join them, or was the party only for the "machos." Their surprise that I knew the slangy local connotation of "blowout" (*reventon* in Spanish) was obvious. They were delighted that I spoke their language and said of course I could join them.

As I got to know the men individually, they loosened up considerably. I made it very clear to all concerned that I had deep respect for and interest in the culture and future well-being of Mexico. In many instances I asked for their "expert" opinion even when I knew the answer. It was a constructive way of showing my involvement with them rather than just with the procedures at hand.

The men I worked with had an insatiable thirst for consumer products from the United States, but an ambivalent attitude toward the American people. Many Mexicans are convinced that U.S. goods are superior to those manufactured in Mexico and proudly show off their U.S. purchases, while at the same time often being angry at U.S. "imperialist policy." Thus the ambivalence toward consultants from the United States. I was able to overcome much ill-feeling by showing that I like and respect the Mexican culture enough to study it and incorporate it into my way of doing business.

When I was sent to Brazil to meet with government, bank and trade association officials, I was anxious at first because my Portuguese was poor. I was delighted to learn, during my many meetings, that in Rio de Janeiro and São Paulo, English is often the language of international business. Quite unlike Mexico, Brazil has a positive, mostly nonambivalent admiration for the United States. Perhaps the sheer size of the country or its distance from the United States is responsible. While few of the offices I visited had women staff members other than secretaries, one of the main exporters' associations had a well-educated professional woman as the assistant to the president.

At each meeting I was offered a cup of the thick, strong coffee that Brazil is so famous for, always served black, along with a glass of ice water. I accepted each time. By the end of the day, I had drunk enough coffee to float home on, but I never refused a cup, nor neglected to comment on the exquisite flavor.

Although I had corresponded with the people I met with for weeks before the meetings, I spent a good deal of time talking about the beauty of the local scenery, the gentility of the people and the economic progress that had been made. My clients all spoke English in varying degrees but were all anxious to practice it with me. I encouraged them, wishing I could speak Portuguese as well. In many instances, English is the second language studied at school and in some Brazilian schools studying English is mandatory!

Brazilians are for the most part an agreeable, pleasant and intelligent people. The meetings had a fairly slow pace in Rio de Janeiro and a more pressured quality in São Paulo. There were more lower-management women in the offices of my clients in São Paulo, but still not terribly many overall. The climate is also somewhat more conducive to business in temperate São Paulo than in tropical Rio. One of my business lunches in Rio in a huge old clublike building lasted for almost three hours. In São Paulo lunch was an affair of a little over an hour in a slick glass and chrome *nouvelle cuisine* restaurant, where my client apologized for the slow service.

My meetings were primarily to set the stage for future dealings in the areas of import/export and countertrade (a form of barter), and were very successful. Probably because I sincerely showed that I wanted to begin a long-term commercial relationship with Brazilian companies and agencies, appointments were set up for me with various Brazilian branch offices in the United States. My relationships with some of my clients continue to this day.

In a recent business trip to England, I had the opportunity to meet with a group of United Kingdom Business and Professional Women, who were hosting a party for a visiting group of executives from New York's Financial Women's Association. (The FWA women were being feted for a week by various British hosts and groups.) Fortunately, I was on assignment in London during the time of the receptions and as an FWA member, I was invited to participate. While there were exceptions, the majority of the British women were somewhat older and less educated than their New York counterparts. Many of the British women were owners of their own businesses. There are few women at the level of manager and above in most British corporations.

One reception was held by the young members of the all-male London Bond Club for the bankers, lawyers and managers that make up the membership of the Financial Women's Association. When asked to comment on the incidence of women in business and professional capacities in the United Kingdom, one member remarked that, "We have a few women like you [FWA] but we're really just beginning to see them." Another fellow, goodnaturedly overwhelmed by the biographical histories of the FWA members, said to me upon being introduced, "Oh my God, are you another financial vice president?" Nevertheless, the admiration for the FWA membership was evident.

My clients in London were of long standing so there was no need for a lengthy getting-to-know-you period. They are top management of a large sophisticated corporation with branch offices in the United States, and had dealt extensively with women managers.

My attendance at a trade show was somewhat less enjoyable. Few women attended and fewer women exhibited. In all fairness, however, U.K. industrial trade shows are pretty much the same as those in the United States. There are still few women present except at computer-related shows. (Computers are a fairly new industry, so women have a relatively higher profile.) The United Kingdom seems to be where the United States was, regarding high-level executive women, roughly 10–15 years ago.

Although equality for women may be far off in many parts of the world, there is almost no country in which a woman executive from the United States cannot succeed if she is patient, prepared and professional.

8

Global Marketing

If one half of the formula for success overseas is to know all you can about your client's market, the other half is to know how to sell in that market. This means you have to know the people you'll be dealing with; and you have to know how to present your product to the country you'll be selling to. The first step is to learn everything about your product, service or deal. The women who are most successful are the ones who, in addition to learning cultural norms, take the time to become expert in their field. Superficial knowledge of what you're peddling isn't enough in the competitive world market. Many clients know a great deal more about your products or services than you may think. You must be prepared to field the most obscure questions about specifications, payment, performance, warranty and contractual obligations—for starters.

Additionally, in many parts of the world it is essential to have at least one local partner on your team. If you are negotiating for a large contract or attempting to enter a major new market, this could be the best, fastest and often only way to succeed. This partner is the key to "market intelligence" that may be unavailable through traditional market research efforts.

In Asia, entering into a business agreement has been likened to joining a family. With careful investigation of the ethics and financial abilities of your potential partner, you can become a presence in the Asian market in a fairly short time. If you are selling consumer products or services, having an Asian partner or advisor can be invaluable. Asian tastes are often very far from what Americans think is attractive, palatable or useful.

For example, goods or services that reflect the U.S. obsession with youth are probably less marketable in Asian societies that admire the wisdom that comes with age. This of course is an obvious difference. There are many subtle differences in consumer behavior that few U.S. businesspeople know about.

Having a partner is not only a shortcut to market entry and a source of market intelligence, but in the Arab world, it is probably the *only* way to negotiate a large project. Negotiations in the Middle East also take a good deal of time and while women can be very successful, it certainly helps (for both men and women) to have an Arab partner on your team. If your company is interested in establishing a presence in the Arab world, you must be prepared to put up with the peculiarities of doing business there. Who else but a local partner would know if the product's packaging or ad campaign are politically "sensitive" or offend a Moslem religious practice.

A local partner need not be a major stockholder in your company. A reputable firm or individual can be hired on a project, contingency, percentage or per diem basis. Think of the difference a local marketing research firm would have made to a U.S. canned soup company that bombed in certain Latin American countries. They could have told the manufacturer that a packaged bouillon cube sold as a soup starter allowed traditional women to feel they were "cooking" something nutritious for their families and that canned soup didn't feel "cooked" to these women. The European manufacturer of powdered and cubed soup bases is still doing very well and the U.S. company lost a great deal of money and withdrew from the market.

There has been a good deal of debate over the validity of "global" goods that are sold everywhere with the same formula and packaging. While there is great similarity in consumer tastes in the major urban centers of the world, less than 20 percent of the population of the developing world lives in these urban areas. Two thirds of the world's total population is found in the developing countries. So while global brands certainly have a place, they are somewhat limited to cosmopolitan centers such as São Paulo, Lagos, Cairo, Seoul and the developed world. It is in these great centers that the homogenizing effects of media and money have created global markets. Electric typewriters, frozen dinners and designer cookies probably won't find a large market in most of the Sudan.

Global marketing strategies tend to work fairly well with mature low-cost items like soft drinks, cosmetics, transistor radios, cigarettes and jeans. The most famous examples of these are Marlboro and Coca-Cola. At the other end of the spectrum, high-priced items can often be sold with global campaigns. Diamonds, expensive Scotch and top-of-the-line automobiles often use a fairly standard approach in their marketing.

While global marketing and advertising save a great deal of money by standardization, it is dangerous to attempt to sell most products or services on a global basis. Global marketing usually includes global advertising: one basic campaign is used throughout the world. But many countries have strict prohibitions on certain forms of advertising that may interfere with a global marketing strategy. For example, in the United Kingdom, even the Marlboro cowboy has been prohibited. Government health officials feel it is dangerous to show heroic figures in cigarette ads because they might encourage people to smoke.

In many countries, comparative claims in advertising aren't allowed; in some, children are not permitted to endorse products on television. Of course, there has been an almost worldwide push to restrict advertising of cigarettes, liquor, violent toys and some drugs in all media.

Obviously though, the greatest problem with global marketing is the cultural difference between people. While shampoo is pretty much shampoo throughout the world, the advertiser must be sure that racial and ethnic differences, time, locale and regional preferences are all taken into consideration. An ad showing a blond-haired model washing her hair at night with shampoo smelling of carnations might bomb miserably in an Asian country where the women all have dark hair, wash their hair in the morning and where carnations signify death or mourning.

Global marketing is even more difficult for services than it is for consumer goods. Law and accounting firms must research their markets very carefully to determine the extent of litigation, the tax structure and the financial reporting procedures of each country in order to fit their services to that country. In fact, in some countries, foreigners are completely barred from rendering legal, accounting, medical and other professional services. Other countries permit foreign professionals to practice only if they pass a local licensing examination and if the local licensing officials approve their foreign degrees. Banks and other financial service companies must understand the makeup of the savings, loan and investment market in relation to consumer behavior.

Whatever type of company you represent, whether dealing in consumer goods, services or industrial projects or products, you cannot go wrong in over-researching your market. The object of your research is to avoid all the costly blunders that have become a part of marketing history and folklore: selling women's razors in those European countries where women don't shave, pushing deodorant to men in countries like Italy and the Philippines where only a small percentage of men use it, offering things in packages of four in Japan where four is the number of death, selling doormats to wipe shoes in Japan where people remove their shoes before entering their homes, or using an ad showing a woman making a major purchase alone in countries where the traditional family structure is still powerful.

Once you know your product and research the culture of your target market you will be able to tell if there is a proper fit. If you are not sure of a fit, you may have to adapt your goods or services to the culture. Very often this can be accomplished by minor modifications.

There are many countries in the world where products must be changed to conform to the legal and economic requirements of the local market. Some of these requirements include converting to the metric system, changing the size and shape of the package, and labeling. Aside from legally required changes, you may find that you have to tailor your product's flavor or fragrance to regional preferences. Canada Dry Co. makes 14 different flavors of orange soda for differing tastes throughout the world. Or, you may have to replace original product contents with local materials to please the host government, lower the price to please the consumer or add protective packaging for hot, humid climates (Quaker Oats uses vacuum tins in the tropics).

Some product features are often inappropriate for particular regions. In some developing countries, dietetic features of foods such as eliminating salt and sugar would be ridiculed. Consumers in those countries want their salt and sugar and don't want to be cheated out of valuable nutrients. Similarly, a bank that advertises free gifts if a customer brings in a new depositor may fail in a country where people never discuss personal finances with each other. In the developing world, usage instructions may have to be modified for less literate consumers. Pictures and movies are often used to instruct consumers in those countries.

Brand names are the subject of a long history of expensive bloopers. Everyone knows the hilarious error made by General Motors when it called its new model Nova and test-marketed it in Latin America: "No va" means "it doesn't go" in Spanish, and the car bombed spectacularly in Latin America until its name was changed to Caribe. Ford didn't fare much better with its truck targeted to the developing world. In certain Latin American countries the name "Fiera" means "ugly old woman." Citibank in Japan was often pronounced "She-tee-bank" until the problem was overcome by the choice of a written character to pronounce the word correctly. In many cases, translations are not enough, and total rewriting may be necessary.

Sometimes, the design of a product is unsuitable for a certain market, regardless of the packaging, advertising and product name. There is a great market in the developing world for refrigerators, water pumps and heavy farm equipment. In many of the rural areas, however, there is erratic or no electricity to drive these products. A company that would produce solar-powered refrigerators, windmill-driven water pumps and pedal-powered farm equipment could make a fortune. Even in areas where there is electricity many countries do not have skilled technicians to operate sophisticated equipment. One major way for you to win large sales and contracts for your company is to show the home office how *less* sophisticated equipment could be sold profitably and how existing equipment could be modified. For example, a truck designed for U.S. highway use can be redesigned for the deserts of Africa or the rainforests of South America. Another way to sell sophisticated equipment in a developing country would be to offer to train mechanics and workers in the use of the products.

Success in many overseas markets means developing or modifying products to the needs of that market. This means employing the marketing concept rather than the sales concept. The sales concept says, "Here is the product, where can we sell it?" While the marketing concept says, "What does the consumer need and how can we produce it?"

A major error often made by U.S. marketers is treating Europe like part of the domestic market, simply because it is part of the developed world. While a fairly high standard of living is enjoyed by most people throughout Europe, there are vast differences in the levels of development. The upper and middle classes show similar consumer behavior patterns throughout the Common Market, but new entrants to the Common Market such as Spain and Portugal still lag behind the Northern countries in purchasing power.

Another error is treating all of Europe as if it were one country. There is no European consumer as such. Your overall marketing strategies for London would be somewhat different from those in the outlying areas of the United Kingdom and quite different from those aimed at the Portuguese farmer or Greek fisherman. Tastes differ widely throughout Europe, as the U.S. manufacturers of Tang orange drink found out. Orange juice and drink are preferred unsweetened in the United Kingdom; even the fresh orange juice served in Britain would be considered bitter by the U.S. consumer. When Tang was reformulated for the British palate, it sold well. The product had trouble in Germany, too, but due to its name, not taste. When a German word was substituted, sales increased.

Europeans like products such as ketchup, mustard, mayonnaise and salad dressings in toothpaste-like tubes. This seems strange to Americans, but U.S. companies interested in selling dressings and condiments should repackage their products for mass market consumption in Europe. There are always specialty shops where glass jars of foods imported from the U.S. will sell because of the mystique or curiosity value of imports, but for the European lower and middle classes, it's dressing in tubes!

Nestlé, the huge Swiss coffee maker, sells its products in every country in the non-Communist world, but makes different coffees for different countries based on taste preferences. The Nescafé in Switzerland tastes very different from the Nescafé in France. The advertising for these coffees is also keyed to local tastes.

Japan is a large consumer of U.S. goods, although to look at the imbalance of trade between Japan and the United States you wouldn't think so. Changing tastes and Westernization have opened up a vast consumer market in that country. McDonalds flourishes in Japan.

By the same token, the United States is a great consumer of Japanese goods. The Japanese have become the largest competitor of the United States, particularly in electronic equipment and in many other consumer products. In the 1950s and 1960s Japanese goods were considered a joke and destined to fall apart as soon as you got them home. In less than 25 years Japanese goods have become synonymous with quality and compete ferociously with those from the United States and Germany for markets in the developed and developing worlds.

While there is tremendous consumer demand for U.S. goods in Japan, there are still tariff and nontariff barriers to sale of those goods. The United States continually threatens to (and occasionally does) impose quotas on Japanese goods, and Japan continually promises to open up its markets. But for companies that persevere, the Japanese market is a most lucrative one. U.S. firms can and do succeed in Japan, despite barriers to entry.

The problem of protectionism is not limited to Japan. Brazil and Mexico have very stringent rules protecting their computer and electronics industries. While the state of those industries is far behind the United States and not at all cost-efficient, Brazil does not allow imports of foreign computers. Mexico has just (in 1985) opened its doors to IBM on a wholly owned basis. The exception to the 51 percent Mexican–49 percent other-owned joint venture laws has been made for Big Blue. Perhaps other companies will now be able to enter the Mexican market in what seems to be a renewed interest in foreign investment there.

Many countries in the developing world, particularly in Latin America, want U.S. goods and services. Most recently, however, the strength of the dollar has made it prohibitive for them to buy from the United States. Harsh financing and credit terms, and demand for payment in dollars, often result in Latin Americans purchasing goods from Europe, Japan or one of the Southeast Asian newcomers. Taiwan, Singapore, South Korea and Hong Kong have become aggressive competitors and are producing high-quality goods at low prices. Let's not forget the way Japan penetrated the Latin American telecommunications market in the 1960s. Although the Latin Americans were ostensibly satisfied with the U.S. products they had been purchasing, they switched to Japanese suppliers because Japan sold products that were comparable to (or only slightly below) the U.S. goods in quality at more reasonable prices. Low price combined with a distinct ability to "massage" the purchasing executives brought strong sales for the Japanese. They unquestionably understood their product and their markets.

Consumer and industrial markets are continually changing and expanding. While the U.S., European and Japanese youth population is declining, the developing world has huge youth market potential. Similarly, the "gray" market of older, affluent consumers in Europe and Japan is a thriving one. Adapt, modify, package, promote and then go out and make a deal!

9

Your Power Presence

"Being a foreigner is so weird to the Japanese, that the marginal impact of being a woman is nothing," says a female personnel vice president of Bank of America's Asia Division. While being a foreigner is not nearly so unusual in some of the less homogeneous societies of other Asian, European and Latin American countries, being a U.S. businesswoman in these places will almost always capture everyone's attention. Nonetheless, the reaction is very often positive. As a businesswoman you are seen much more as a "foreign executive" who happens to be a woman than as a "woman" who has a more traditional role in the local society. Especially in developing countries, the fact that you *look* different from the locals helps your clients to see you as "executive," not as "woman."

Upon hearing that I was waiting for my scheduled meeting in the reception area, one of the Brazilian central bankers I was to meet said in Portuguese, "Did you say Mister Rossman is a woman?" He had not, in our earlier correspondences by telex and mail, realized that I was a woman. As I understood enough Portuguese to realize his surprise, my gut knotted at the prospect of dealing with what I assumed to be strong prejudice. When he emerged to greet me a minute later, I was prepared to be defensive and stood stiffly while shaking hands. To my surprise, he was warm and friendly, and told me that it hadn't occurred to him that I was a woman. He had assumed (correctly) that anyone he was dealing with had to be on a high level and (incorrectly) would therefore be a man. In order to allow him to save face, I did not point out that my name could rarely be mistaken for a man's (even though I routinely get mail from overseas addressed to me as "Mister"). I did mention that I had come up with a new idea to generate Brazilian export credits. His interest and excitement over my suggestion was so strong that after formalities and coffees we worked for four hours. He never mentioned the fact of my being a woman again.

The Brazilian banker's surprise at finding I was a woman was by no means an isolated incident. Nevertheless, after the shock wore off, my clients at other Latin American meetings were, for the most part, amenable to doing business with me. My knowledge of and experience in each country had much to do with my being accepted.

The best way to overcome initial resistance is to show your expertise at the first appropriate occasion. You want to be judged on your ability and skill, not on the basis of sex.

When you enter a meeting room, stand tall even if you're only five feet tall. Your height is unimportant; it's your posture that gives clues about your general feeling toward yourself and your expertise. The first impression will tell your client either that you are in control and self-confident or that you are anxious and unsure. If you don't feel confident, fake it. Shake hands firmly or bow as the formalities dictate. If you have been delayed and arrive late, don't rush in apologizing while gasping for air. Arriving late in many countries is appropriate. When late in Europe, simply compose yourself and apologize briefly.

While it is important to behave, dress and carry yourself like the executive you are, it is not necessary to clone yourself into a gray flannel neuter. What does the businesswoman wear to set off her powerful presence? Never a floppy bow tie! A totally "male" dress style is never appropriate. Beyond this one generality, clothes should vary with the temperature and personality of the place. For example, in Rio de Janeiro, Brazil, a good cotton, silk or linen blend dress is appropriate. In São Paulo, an hour away from Rio by air, a light gray, taupe, peach or other soft-colored suit is your best bet. In the tropical informal bikinied atmosphere of Rio, a suit is not only uncomfortable but stuffy looking. In the more temperate, business-oriented climate of São Paulo, a suit is appropriate, but a dark suit would be too somber for the Brazilian personality.

You can wear your navy blue suit in places that have a cold climate, stress conformity and formality or have a strong U.S. orientation. In many parts of Europe, your navy blue suit and a colorful soft blouse are excellent choices. Your gray and navy suits worn with a good blouse are the proper uniform for Japan, too. Avoid slacks and heavily starched man-tailored blouses. You can wear dresses in most places if you are more comfortable.

Take a blazer along if you want a jacket for warmth or for a more powerful look. Well-cut silk, wool or cotton dresses are appropriate anywhere.

Save sandals, heavy makeup, long glamorous hair, strong perfume, sheer blouses, heavy jewelry and large purses for a nonbusiness event. You do not want your clients to be distracted from your purposes—negotiating and closing the deal. You want to look attractive, not seductive or unprofessional.

Recent studies at Yale, New York University and other universities have shown that being attractive has negative consequences for executive women. However, being attractive is considered an advantage for men. Some researchers have gone so far as to say that women should try to appear as unattractive and masculine as possible if they want to succeed in their careers. More moderate researchers have suggested that very attractive women should seek to "play down" their attractiveness if they want to be judged on their ability.

Don't worry about playing down your femininity with your overseas client—you are not competing with him, nor are you his wife, date, daughter or friend. You can look attractive as long as your bearing shouts "professional." There is nothing that states that purpose better than a solid-color well-cut, below-the-knee suit skirt or dress, mid-high-heel pumps, neutral panty hose and a gentle but firm handshake.

If you have very long hair, pull it away from your face in a French twist or knot. You don't have to look unfeminine, just businesslike. Short to medium length hair should also be combed away from the face. Avoid colorful barrettes and dangling earrings. One good piece of jewelry, like a pin or a strand of pearls, points up your good taste.

I usually do not carry a briefcase on overseas trips, although I always carry one in the United States. If I don't need to go over my papers on the plane trip, I put them in a "Redweld" legal size expandable cardboard folder and pack them in my suitcase or carry-on bag. Although I don't carry a purse with my briefcase at home, I wear a good leather shoulder strap purse overseas. But if you need your briefcase on your trip, don't carry a purse, too. Put a small clutch purse into your briefcase for your personal items, and carry it on board the plane. You don't want to arrive at a meeting overburdened. Picture yourself fumbling with a heavy briefcase, an umbrella, a purse, address directions and possibly a map. I like the shoulder purse and Redweld combination because I tuck the folder under my arm and both my hands are free. Also, with the Redweld packed, I have one less piece of luggage to worry about.

Of course, to find out the best way to put yourself together, observe the locals. The problem with this is that you have to pack before you get there. The next best thing is to find out about the climate of the place along with the degree of traditionalism. In the Middle East, for example, if you are working in Saudi Arabia, be prepared to take calf-length midi-skirts and long-sleeve loose-fitting blouses along. Or you could purchase the loose-flowing ankle-length dress that Arab women wear. You do not need to wear a veil under any circumstances, but you may be more comfortable in the fashionable long dress that has been called "Koran chic" in honor of the re-vival of the fundamentalist dictates of the Islamic religion. In less conser-vative places like Egypt, Jordan, Bahrain and the United Arab Emirates, a woman can comfortably wear a plain suit or dress. Of course, in Israel a woman can wear whatever she wishes, although a light-colored loose cot-ton garment is most comfortable for the climate.

Although most synthetic fabrics don't wrinkle, they retain body heat and often look cheap. A blend of 65 percent linen and 35 percent polyester however looks beautiful, doesn't wrinkle much and breathes. I usually travel with a few silk/cotton blend blouses ordered from a catalog, that can be washed in a hotel sink and hung up to dry on a padded hanger. These blouses need little or no ironing if you hang them to dry carefully. After a number of bad experiences dry cleaning my silk blouses in Latin America, I now try to avoid having my clothes cleaned anywhere in the world. The silk/cotton blend blouses are reasonably priced, luxurious and Woolite washable. Best of all, you can keep your anxiety level down by rinsing them out with your pantyhose.

No matter what blouses or dresses you wear, be sure they cover the en-tire neck area. The "neck dimple" is a vulnerable area and a subliminal sign of invitation—not necessarily a sexual invitation, so much as a sign of harmlessness and lack of power. If need be, drape a scarf around your neck.

So you are beautifully dressed, poised, confident and the negotiations have gone well. What about taking your client to lunch or dinner? You hesi-tate. So much has been written on power lunching in the United States (Who picks up the check? Where to go? What to drink?) that it seems like an insurmountable task, even compared to the exhausting negotiating you've just been through. In fact, it's probably easier to accomplish a "power" lunch with your overseas client than at home, where you might lose points for eating sushi or quiche. If you have the opportunity before you go, read up on the food of the country. Don't hesitate to ask someone for a restaurant recommendation or have your client pick out a favorite res-taurant and make a reservation. Don't worry about your power presence at lunch or dinner, you've already shown your authority and ability at the meeting. The United States is one of the few countries in the world where business deals are made over a meal. In most places lunch or dinner is a place to relax a bit and enjoy. So don't continue discussing the business deal once you arrive at the restaurant. Knowledge of music, art and literature is highly respected in most countries. Your college liberal arts courses will come in handy here.

One of the most useful things you *can* do during lunch is to draw your client out and learn things about him and his country. One way to begin is to ask about his family. Everywhere in the world except Saudi Arabia and other very traditional Arab countries, questions about family are welcomed. While it is unlikely that you will be asked to dine with a Saudi Arabian client, if you do, keep the conversation to the climate and the technological advances of the country.

Avoid trying to look into a Saudi's eyes. In the United States, someone who doesn't look you in the eye seems suspicious, but in Saudi Arabia and other very traditional Arab countries it may be considered hostile or worse, intimate. In Japan it is considered rude to look someone deeply in the eyes. Try to be conscious of your habit of gazing deeply into the eyes. Arabs often wear dark glasses so you won't be able to see the changes in their pupils that give away vital information. Outside of Western Europe and Latin America, try to gaze less directly at your client.

If your client asks you about your family, tell him briefly. Before I was married, I routinely invented a fiancé to forestall comments about what a shame it is that I was alone. By skillfully asking your client about his family you can learn a great deal. Avoid giving out a lot of information about yourself.

Another topic of conversation is the client's country. Tell him, for instance, that you are interested in a specific city, and he will probably give you a short travelogue. Think of how informed you'll sound for your next client when you discuss the virtues of San Flores. Even if you only have time to skim a travel guide to your client's country, pick out something in which you are genuinely interested and ask your client to tell you about it. Your client will think you a well-informed and intelligent individual. People all over the world love to talk about their favorite subject, themselves. Given the opportunity, they will respond informatively to questions such as "What music and arts do you enjoy?" or "What parts of your country do you like best?" Avoid controversial subjects like the status of local women in business, if you want a pleasant meal.

If your client urges you to talk about yourself, give anecdotes about the United States in general and your city in particular. My clients love to hear about apartment prices in New York, and about the city's dangers, cultural activities and its incredibly fast pace. No matter where you live, stories about the United States fascinate people from all over. If you can laugh at some of the idiosyncrasies of the United States, you will feel at ease and also put your client at ease. Then you can settle down to the real business at hand, enjoying your meal.

While you may have read guidelines against ordering certain foods at a "power lunch," lest your prestige be diminished, there is a growing movement in the United States for even the most macho of business executives to eat lightly. I had lunch recently with the head of worldwide marketing of one of the largest financial services companies in the United States. He ordered a turkey sandwich, cole slaw, mineral water and fresh fruit for dessert. Hardly the stuff of power lunching, right? Wrong! The trend toward fitness and coronary health has led many men away from heavy, rich food. There is a movement among U.S. executives to live long enough to enjoy their six-figure incomes.

Most high-power executives overseas are not eating turkey sandwiches and cole slaw for lunch, however, and neither would you. For one thing, you would probably have to go to the American Club or a U.S.-style restaurant for it, and unless you are certain your client likes U.S.-style food, you are better off having lunch on your client's turf. Remember, a meal is not a struggle for supremacy, just pure enjoyment, and part of the enjoyment of travel is trying the local cuisine.

One rule of thumb is that when inland, avoid ordering seafood, especially in the developing world. Broiled meats and chicken are excellent choices. If you are in a coastal area anywhere in the world, you will probably enjoy the seafood most. But avoid raw shellfish everywhere in the developing world. In most of South America, beef is prized. It is grass-fed rather than grain-fed, and cut differently than in the United States. If you have never tasted steak like the kind served in Buenos Aires, Argentina or São Paulo, Brazil, you are in for a treat. It is less fatty than U.S. beef and sweeter.

In Japan, the beef is also special, and you can order steaks shabu shabu and sukiyaki. In the rest of Asia, take advantage of the superb regional cuisine. Taste Chinese food that is nothing like your corner Cantonese restaurant. Here is your opportunity to have real Thai food, Indonesian rijstaffel, Malaysian satays and Indian curries.

By all means, order mineral water. It was drunk by everyone, everywhere in the world long before the United States discovered Perrier. Since tap water may be less than reliable outside the United States, everyone drinks bottled water with meals.

Even if you don't enjoy drinking, order something alcoholic, if only to toast your client and his country. You don't have to drink much, or finish the beverage, but it is part of the social ritual.

Although I enjoy a drink before dinner or wine with dinner, I find it difficult to drink during lunch. Probably due to the fact that I equate having a drink with my leisure time, I can't return to work after lunch-hour drinking. In the United States I simply don't order alcohol. When I am overseas I always order beer or a glass of wine during lunch, even if I don't drink much of it. Once, during some particularly sticky negotiations in the Dominican Republic, I invited my client to lunch. Knowing that in that country, as in all the Caribbean, drinking expensive imported Scotch is a status symbol, even though the local rum is superb, I ordered Scotch whisky. My client, a self-important macho and somewhat difficult individual, was surprised and blurted out, "But that's a real man's drink!" I replied that I loved the aroma and taste of good Scotch. (As it happens, I do, but not at lunch.) He was so impressed that he didn't even notice how little of it I drank. Although situations like this are exceptions, the usual rule of thumb is to order whatever beverage the country is famous for. The beer is superb in Germany, Holland and most of the developing world. Wine is magnificent in Italy, France, Spain, Chile and Argentina. Whiskeys are excellent in the United Kingdom. When I am in Puerto Rico on business, my favorite after dinner drink is a little-known aged, dark rum that is exported in small quantities. It is a rich cognac-like spirit produced in small batches by Ron Barrilito. I doubt that I have won any contracts by ordering it, but the fact that I know of it certainly does impress my clients.

At the end of your meal when you and your client both reach for the check say, "Please allow me the honor of buying you lunch (or dinner)." If he puts up a fight or argues loudly, allow him to pick up the check and ask for a return engagement when you can buy him a meal. Or if your language ability is excellent or the management speaks English, politely ask the captain to give you the check. This should be done during a trip to the telephone or washroom. Whatever happens, don't try to explain you are on expense account, and don't argue with your client for the check. That's where a real loss of power can occur. If you feel uncomfortable about not paying for the meal, or fear he will not allow you to pick up the check, send him a small impersonal gift, like an appliance, book or ashtray, along with your business card and a thank-you note.

Aside from lunch, dinner or a drink, you may not enjoy socializing with your overseas clients. There are some exceptions, however, when socializing is part of the business ritual. In Japan, it is quite common for people to go out and drink in the evening. If you feel this ritual is part of the requirement of doing business, by all means, participate in it. Eat beforehand and match toasts but try to drink as little as possible. At best you'll be hung over and at worst your tongue will loosen so that you will regret what you said, even if you didn't give out any industrial secrets. But in Japan it is considered bad form to repeat or use to advantage what others have said while under the influence of alcohol. When others are drinking, they rarely count how many you've had, so go in the spirit of friendship, but go easy with the spirits.

Part of establishing your power presence includes knowing little things about the country you're dealing in. You gain a tremendous advantage by surprising your client with things that he thinks are known only within the boundaries of that country. Knowing a word in the language, a dish that is famous, a part of the country that is regarded with pride are some of the things that can make you stand out from the competition. While you do not want to try to become someone from his country (you lose your mystique and advantage), you must learn as much as you can about the culture, and play by those rules.

As a woman you have a tremendous advantage. You are an unknown quantity. One of my clients in Milan lit up like a Christmas tree when he saw that M. Rossman was a woman and spoke some Italian. He said he was expecting a tall man in a baggy suit and heavy oxfords who couldn't pronounce his name, wore a college ring and shook his hand so hard that the crest of the ring imprinted on his finger. Since it was the first time he had dealt professionally with a businesswoman from the United States, he seemed a little uncertain about how to treat me. The attitudes and rules that he went by when doing business with a U.S. businessman obviously didn't seem right to him, nor did he seem inclined to behave toward me the way Italian men behave toward Italian women. I could sense his confusion. I didn't rush to open the door for myself, insist that he not stand up when I came into a room and most of all didn't scream at him when he told me, "It was a pleasure to do business with an attractive lady." All of the things that irritated me in the United States seemed somehow natural in Italy. I couldn't afford to become sidetracked with little irritations. The guidelines that we all follow in the United States aren't valid overseas. Use this to your advantage, take the lead and make up the rules for yourself and your client—that's real power!

10

Life on the Road

There is a tremendous mystique surrounding an overseas trip, even when (often especially when) it's for business. Your friends are envious, your husband or partner is jealous, your parents are nervous (what will my little girl do all alone in Hong Kong?), while you are making exciting arrangements for your meetings. Rewarding? Yes! But glamorous? No! Think of the "glamour" of stumbling off a plane jet-lagged, having been bored to tears by a garrulous seatmate during your 14-hour flight and having to go to a meeting in two hours. Even more "glamorous" is trying to negotiate a deal with a dyed-in-the-wool believer in keeping women barefoot and pregnant, who is offering you endless cups of coffee while you're suffering from a case of *turista*.

Certainly, business travel can be glamorous at times, and there are ways to minimize the discomforts. But even at the worst moments, remember that you are doing this for the future of your career, so pack your eye drops and Lomotil, follow the jet-lag diet, peel your vegetables—and knock 'em dead!

Whether you are exhausted, suffering from stomach problems or just plain disoriented, don't let on as it might have a bad impact on your dealings. When Secretary of State George Schultz met with Andrei Gromyko a while back, Mr. Gromyko asked casually if Mr. Schultz was travel weary. Mr. Schultz, wisely realizing that revealing a weakness could disadvantage his negotiations, said he had slept on the plane. Whether or not he slept is unimportant. What mattered is that he did not reveal any information that could have been used against him.

You can do many things to counteract jet lag, illness and lack of sleep. If you are traveling to Europe or South America and have the luxury of a day flight, take advantage of it. You can go to sleep when you arrive and be fresh for the next day's business. When booking your flight, be aware of the fact that on most airlines, you can get your boarding pass, or at least a seat assignment, up to 30 days before you fly. If you travel business or first class there are lounges to wait in before the flight. If you are a frequent flyer, you can often use bonus points to upgrade your seat to first class. All of this is designed to cut down on the standing on line, rushing and crowding in the airport that can increase your exhaustion.

Because of the long time needed to fly to the Far East, along with the added disorientation that comes from crossing the international date line, you should allow yourself one full day to adjust, if possible. Many corporations are becoming aware of the importance of adjusting your circadian rhythms (body clock) to the locale. They encourage executives flying long distances to change their diets and schedules to maximize success in negotiating.

Many experienced travelers swear by the "jet lag diet," a four-day regimen of controlled eating and drinking which is supposed to help your body adjust to changes in time zones. The details of this diet have been reported in the travel sections of many newspapers and magazines. If you are the type who suffers badly from jet lag, or if you are taking a flight that will carry you across many time zones (such as flying from New York to Tokyo, a difference of 14 hours), you might want to investigate this diet.

If this diet seems too much trouble to follow, or if you don't have four days in which to follow it (for example, if you are given an emergency assignment and your meeting is on the next day), you can still minimize the effect of jet lag. The most important thing is to avoid caffeine and alcohol on the flight. While it's tempting to drink coffee or cocktails on the plane (or both), alcohol and caffeine are the two substances that cause the worst symptoms of jet lag. Your body is prone to dehydration in the desert-dry atmosphere of an airplane, and caffeine and alcohol compound the problem. Drink lots of juices and water. Eat lightly and try to nap. You can order special meals on most airlines at no extra cost. Try the fruit plate or the vegetarian meal. Besides being lighter and more healthful, they are, in many cases, the best-tasting food you can order. Another good bet is the low-sodium dinner, which also helps to fight dehydration because it lacks the excessive salt common to typical airline food. Low-sodium, fruit and vegetarian meals also usually come with fresh fruit instead of the dessicated, overly sweet desserts that the regular airline meals feature.

Try to sleep on the plane, or at least close your eyes and rest. Picture what people are doing at your destination and set your watch to that time. Buy a sleep mask and use it. If nothing else, it may help to discourage seatmates who are anxious to talk. If your flight isn't full, find a row of empty seats, get some pillows and a blanket, and stretch out. On a flight to Peru that was interrupted by a landing in Miami for minor repairs, I slept for an hour in a row of seats, and read and rested the remainder of the trip. Although I was on the plane for over 14 hours, I felt relatively refreshed when I arrived.

If you have an interesting seatmate and wish to talk, do so but not for the entire flight. You'll most likely be staying in the same city so you can meet the next day if you want.

If you haven't had the chance to read extensively about the country you'll be working in, this is the time. Take a paperback along that deals with the culture of the country. Try to avoid business reading at this time, if you can. If you're looking for a little escape reading, a spy or romantic novel might be just the thing: If it's a well-written novel, it will help to pass the time; if it's bad it might help you fall asleep! Sometimes you may have to work during your flight. Begin the work when you get on the plane. When you finish you can relax, nap or read a novel.

Packing a few extra paperbacks is a good idea, especially if you are traveling to Southeast Asia, the Middle East or Latin America. You may find the selection in hotel shops limited to two-year-old titles at steep prices. English-language paperbacks are easier to find in most of Europe. Discarding the paperbacks after you've read them lightens your luggage for the return flight, leaving precious space for the gifts you'll be bringing home. You may also want to pack a Walkman and music or language tapes.

Try to pack as little as possible. If you are going on a trip for a short time, take travel sizes of all cosmetics, medications and appliances. Pack cosmetics in breakproof plastic containers. I keep a kit packed with all the shampoo, creams, aspirins, toothpaste and dental floss I need for up to three weeks on the road. It's wonderful for fast and frequent getaways.

Some other travel aids you may want are a mini hair dryer with dual voltage, a set of international electric plugs and/or adapter, a tiny first aid kit, a sewing kit, a Swiss army knife, a travel iron, a portable alarm clock, flashlight and matches, an umbrella, plastic bags, a pocket calculator, packets of Woolite, a camera and film. You can get all of these items in small sizes or quantities. For those traveling in somewhat dangerous areas, or for the overcautious, there are portable door alarms, portable door jambs and deadbolts that can be mail-ordered or purchased from sporting goods and specialty shops in the United States.

Change a few dollars at a foreign exchange bank at home. Sometimes airport banks are crowded or closed when you arrive. Have enough foreign currency with you when you land to tip the airport porter and pay for a cab to your hotel.

Keep all your documents and medications, a few cosmetics and your toothbrush in your carry-on luggage. If your baggage is lost, it's comforting to know you can argue with the airline officials with clean teeth, and with your cash and papers tucked into your tote bag. You can then meet with your client, secure in the knowledge that the airline is doing everything possible to find your bags, and still have clean teeth and fresh lipstick. For the same reason, the directions to the meeting should be carried with you, as should at least the most essential of your business documents.

Packing everything in a garment bag is the best way to cut down on the possibility of lost baggage, and to get to your hotel without waiting for what seems like hours at the baggage carousel. These bags hold an enormous amount of clothing and can be carried onto the plane and hung up in the on-board coat closet.

If you are going to wear suits to your meetings and are staying for up to three weeks, two suits and a contrasting skirt are all you need. The suit jacket can serve as a blazer for the extra skirt. Take tailored blouses for the daytime and dressy ones for evenings. A strapless camisole top made out of silk or linen with a softly tailored suit makes a superb evening outfit. If you have to entertain clients, keep the jacket on; if you are dating or going to a non-business function, you can take the jacket off. Add a dress, some interesting accessories, sports clothing appropriate to the climate and culture of the country and comfortable shoes. All this can be packed into a garment bag. Your other necessities go into a carry-on shoulder tote which also usually holds a tremendous amount. Don't bother with a purse for the trip—you need your hands free to maneuver. If you must have a purse, you can pack a small one in the garment or tote bag.

If you are wearing dresses, take three or four good ones whose looks can be changed by adding costume jewelry, a belt and silk scarf.

Whatever you're wearing, don't overpack. You may want to shop a little during your free time. Western Europe is a particularly good place for U.S. women to buy clothing and accessories. The cut of the clothing often fits without alterations. In the Far East and Latin America, the cut is somewhat less suited to American women, but here too you can buy some good clothing and plenty of beautiful accessories.

No matter where you are, though, you may find an unexpected bargain. On one of my business trips to Rio, I spent my entire free day shopping in the fancy Ipanema boutiques featuring $250 designer dresses, but couldn't find anything that fit me properly. A few days later, I had two hours to kill between meetings, and I wandered into a nearby shopping center. In a very unpretentious women's clothing store, I found a beautiful black cocktail dress hanging on a pipe rack bearing a $30 price tag. It needed only a few alterations to fit me perfectly. The dress always gets compliments when I wear it at New York parties, but I always reply, "This? It's just a little number I picked up in Rio."

Try to have some input into which hotels you'll be staying in, if your company or its travel agent allows. I always try to pick a hotel owned by a U.S., Canadian or major international chain. Staying in a small quaint hotel may be very pleasant in London or Paris, but in the smaller cities of Europe or in the developing world, stick with a large international one. Though often cold and impersonal, these large chains are more used to seeing businesswomen and often offer telexes, photocopying, safe deposit boxes, valets and other business and personal services. Large hotel chains frequently have swimming pools, saunas and exercise rooms as well. Many large hotels can get you a guest pass to a tennis or golf club if you request it. Keep in shape by exercising in your room if your hotel doesn't have any sports or exercise facilities. A businesswoman friend of mine travels with a jump rope and works out with it daily.

If your hotel doesn't provide business and other services, ask the concierge to help you. In most major cities in the world you can get secretarial services, translators, conference rooms and audiovisual equipment. Particularly in the developing world, a small discreet tip to the concierge makes these things happen as if by magic.

Large hotels often have good restaurants and comfortable lounges. I've eaten dinner alone in many high-quality rooftop hotel restaurants around the world. Hotel coffee shops usually offer substantial meals if you want comfort and informality.

You don't have to limit yourself to your hotel, however, unless you're in a small town in the developing world, or in parts of the Middle East. Elsewhere, when you have the time, try the best local restaurants. Ask for a list of good restaurants or look them up in a travel guide and take yourself to one. Dining alone can be one of the most pleasant aspects of a business trip.

Make a reservation, go to the restaurant, order wine and sit back and reflect on how well you've done. A woman friend who never goes to good restaurants alone in New York, where she lives, goes to dinner alone in most of the places she travels to. She feels less out of place dining alone overseas than she does at home.

When you are dining alone you can explore different restaurants. Take your clients to the international establishments—you don't want any surprises. But an unusual dish or drink in a restaurant halfway around the world can be a rare pleasure, to be savored when you're dining alone.

A few years ago, during a particularly stressful round of meetings in Venezuela, I found myself with a completely free weekend. I was staying in Caracas at a large U.S.-owned hotel that had full services and a pool. Saturday, I swam, had an excellent massage, had my hair shampooed in the beauty salon, and ordered a superb dinner and wine from room service. Sunday, I repeated the procedure but went to dinner at a nearby restaurant. By Monday morning I was refreshed and ready to continue my battles. I was able to win the contract for my company, a fact that I partially attribute to my relaxing weekend.

A woman acquaintance spends her free time on business trips dieting. During the evenings that she has dinner with her clients she eats regular meals, but when she is on her own she often goes to a green grocer and brings an assortment of fresh fruit and vegetables back to her room. If you want to try this, travel with a can opener, knife, fork, spoon and cork screw.

When you are on the road for a long period of time, it's a good idea to pamper yourself. Do things that you wouldn't do ordinarily. Although I have never ridden in a hansom cab around Central Park in New York, I rode in one during a stay in Guadalajara, Mexico.

As a woman traveling alone, you may be harassed by that particular assortment of weirdos that are permanent fixtures in every country. Rude or patronizing clerks, porters, waiters, managers, and so on, can be found all over the world. Many hotels in the United States have recently introduced special seminars for instructing their personnel on correct behavior toward female guests. Unfortunately, this is not yet the case in most of the world. At any rate, unpleasant experiences can still happen to you when you're traveling alone, whether you're in New York, St. Louis, Rome or Hong Kong. Men, too, are sometimes treated rudely. Don't hesitate to complain to the management if you are not being treated properly.

When you check in, be conscious of those around you. Take the key and ask for a bellhop. This way you can be sure that the room is ready, and can have the bellhop explain where the electrical outlets and extra blankets are if you need them.

Use caution when depositing and picking up your key. There is no more irritating situation than to receive a phone call from some inebriated character who saw your room number hours earlier when you were picking up your key. All hotels have a security staff. Don't hesitate to use them if you have to.

If you are traveling to a city or region that has had any incidence of kidnaping, terrorism or mugging, use extra caution on the streets and in the hotel. In this case a portable door alarm or door jamb might make sense. Be certain to use only licensed and metered cabs. In most places, however, your usual common sense is enough protection.

Getting sick on your trip during an important series of meetings can be devastating. There is no guarantee against illness but you can cut down on your chances of becoming seriously ill. Many people experience mild discomfort when they travel anywhere, even to another state in the United States, due to the changes in water, climate and altitude. It's normal then to expect some changes when traveling thousands of miles. Some places in the developing world do not have the same sanitary standards as London or Paris, but you can get sick anywhere in the world, even at home.

Check with the Center for Disease Control in Atlanta or the World Health Hotline in your city before you leave. If immunization shots are recommended, take them. The protection is worth the small amount of discomfort. Be especially careful of food and drink in the developing world. Always drink *carbonated* bottled water, because an unscrupulous waiter could fill a bottle with tap water and present it to you as just opened. If you are unsure about the ice cubes, drink your cocktails mixed with chilled juice or sodas, or better yet, drink beer, which is safe everywhere.

As a general rule in the developing world, don't eat uncooked fruit, vegetables or fish. Avoid shellfish, custard fillings, creams and cheeses unless you are sure that they have been properly refrigerated and prepared. Your best bets in the developing world are cooked meats and poultry, soups and stews, rice, potatoes and cooked greens.

If, even after using extreme caution, you become ill, try to avoid self-medicating. Routine traveler's diarrhea, which is painless, mild and lasts from one to three days, is very different from the severe, painful diarrhea that can indicate something more serious. Eat very lightly and avoid dehydration by drinking canned or bottled fruit juice. Soup, tea, bread and crackers, colas, rice and bananas are recommended. If you must attend an important meeting, Lomotil or Kaopectate will lessen the diarrheic episodes temporarily but they don't get rid of the disease. These medications should be used only for emergency situations. An English-speaking doctor in Mexico City once told me that taking these drugs is dangerous because your body can reabsorb the infection. The best thing, he felt, was to let severe diarrhea run its course, while taking antibiotics to prevent infecting the organs.

No matter what the symptoms, if you don't feel well after a day or two, call a doctor. It's a good idea to let the doctor know what medications you are allergic to, if you are taking oral contraceptives or if you have any preexisting medical problems.

Large hotels often have a competent doctor on the staff. There are a number of organizations in the United States that will provide you with a list of English-speaking doctors throughout the world. Try the International Association for Medical Assistance to Travelers (IAMAT) or INTER-MEDIC in New York. Medical insurance is available for travelers as well, so check with your insurer.

Unfortunately, malaria has not been eradicated in some parts of the developing world, and other mosquito-borne illnesses are still prevalent in some countries. If you're traveling to one of these countries, make sure you pack a can of mosquito repellent and if you have any doubts, ask for a mosquito net at your hotel.

Don't be alarmed if your menstrual period is early or late. Flying often upsets the menstrual cycle slightly. Unless you are traveling to Western Europe, Japan or Hong Kong, take along a supply of tampons if you use them. Sanitary napkins are easy to find throughout the world, but tampons are not always easily available in many places. If you anticipate having your menstrual period while traveling, it is comforting to have a supply of tampons in your suitcase.

The same goes for birth control pills, although sometimes they can be obtained in some surprising places. A woman who was traveling in rural Mexico had to stay longer than she anticipated and needed her next month's supply of birth control pills. Worried that as an unmarried American woman she would have a hard time obtaining a supply of pills in a heavily Catholic country, she went to a doctor's office armed with a long sob story about losing her pills and her husband not wanting any more children. Before she got to see the doctor, she tearfully explained her problem in broken Spanish to the receptionist who told her to go next door to the pharmacy to buy the pills. When the woman explained that she didn't have her prescription with her, the receptionist said, "Just go next door and ask for Ovral." She did and got the pills. When she got them back to her hotel room she read the package and saw that they were manufactured in New Jersey!

Nonetheless, some women have had a hard time getting contraceptives in foreign countries, so it's always a good idea to bring along whatever you think you'll need and maybe a little extra.

So, you've prepared for your trip, you've kissed friends, family and lovers good-bye, and you're speeding to your destination. Then what? You certainly have your work and meetings cut out for you, but what will you do on the weekends and evenings that you don't have to work? For the first few days of work, just having dinner will be an effort, but as you adjust to the environment you will want to see people and things, especially if you're lucky enough to be working in a great capital city. Certainly in places like London, Munich, Cairo, Hong Kong and São Paulo, you will have no difficulty finding interesting things to do. Even in smaller "second cities," there will be plenty of culture to absorb. If you are working in a small town, take a plane to the capital or to the nearest beach resort for the weekend and enjoy. Or simply stay in the small town and use this time to catch up on sleep. This is a good opportunity to soak in a tub, have a facial or massage and read a good book. Small towns can be delightful, too, and taking a tour or meeting the people can be a good way to spend time.

Depending on the culture, spending your nonworking time may sometimes be a little more difficult than your working time. Your intelligence and professionalism have convinced your clients that a woman executive can be as good as or better than a man, but out of the business context how are women alone regarded and treated? In most places today, especially in big cities, women alone are accepted, but in some places you may be seen as fair game. Men overseas have gotten used to seeing women tourists alone; but don't be surprised if you are approached by them. Twenty years ago a lone U.S. or British tourist to Spain would have an American flag or Union Jack propped up at her restaurant table to signal the locals that she wasn't a prostitute. Today, you can have lunch or dinner at many formerly all-male preserves without raising an eyebrow.

Socializing in most of Western Europe is somewhat similar to that in the United States. Of course, men will try to flirt with you, but that's nothing new. Latin America is quite a bit behind Western Europe but certainly large cities like Buenos Aires, Rio de Janeiro, São Paulo, Lima, Caracas, Bogotá and Mexico City are fairly comfortable for women travelers. In most of the big cities of the Far East, you can move about with relative ease, save for China and Japan. Activities are carefully monitored in China; and in Japan you'll probably spend a lot of time socializing with your clients as business *is* pleasure there. You won't be able to move around unrestrictedly in much of the Middle East except for Egypt and Israel, but in the Gulf States you will be able to spend quality time with fascinating women.

An excellent way to meet people for single and married women is to spend time with a local family. Although I'm not religious, I have been using *The Jewish Travel Guide,* edited by Sidney Lightman (published in the United Kingdom) for ten years. When I was single and traveling to a new place, I'd write or call one of the congregations listed in this book. I would explain (sometimes in English, sometimes in the language of the country) that I was a young woman, traveling on business and I wanted to meet a local family. To my great delight I almost always received warm and gracious hospitality. For example, I was picked up at the airport in Bogotá by a limousine whose chauffeur insisted that I come to the family's home; invited to a large formal dinner in Mexico City; and introduced to an eligible dentist nephew in São Paulo. These people were as anxious to meet a U.S. woman as I was to meet a local family. While I don't know of any similar publications for other religions, the same effect may be accomplished by contacting the main church headquarters in your home city and asking for a listing of churches in any city overseas. If you're not a church member, try making overseas contacts through your athletic group, chess club or other association. Since I've been married, I still use the same method, only now I refuse dates from eligible young dentists!

Another excellent way to meet people is through professional or university affiliations. I am an alumna of New York University and belong to the NYU Club. The Club has reciprocal privileges at private and university clubs throughout the United States and the world; so do many other U.S. university clubs. Before leaving to work in the United Kingdom, I got a letter of introduction from the NYU Club to the Oxford-Cambridge Club in London. There is little to compare with having a family or superb club welcome you 5,000 miles away from home.

Being lonely while traveling on business is to be expected. Even with an overseas family or newfound club friends, don't be surprised at how much you will miss your family and friends.

What about your love and sex life? If you are married you can go to dinner or a club with your newfound friends, flirt outrageously if you wish and excuse yourself to call your husband. If the time zones aren't too wildly apart, have a sexy conversation with your husband. If you're single and have a lover back home, you can do the same, but you do have other options as well.

If you are interested in a sexual or romantic encounter, you will have little trouble meeting men who are only too happy to accommodate you. Use the same discretion that you would in New York, Chicago, Atlanta or

Dubuque. As a general rule, avoid clients, colleagues and men in bars. Try striking up a conversation with a man in a private club, museum or restaurant, or while sitting at a sidewalk café. Even if your foreign-language ability is limited to asking about the daily quotes on pig iron, you will be able to communicate your interest. Many times you will be approached without even trying. Use your judgment. When I was single, I met a man in the Jockey Club restaurant in Madrid, after the headwaiter brought me his card on a silver tray. The headwaiter assured me of the man's good character and standing in the Spanish business community. I couldn't held thinking about how much the waiter received in tips for his help, but I decided to be bold and sent my admirer *my* business card and told the waiter I'd be delighted to meet him. His English was superb and I found him to be charming and brilliant, but married. Nonetheless, I enjoyed his company during dinner.

Even during your leisure time, keep your business card with you. If you meet an interesting man, you can offer your card and ask for his. A lot of information appears on those cards, especially in Europe. Some people even list their university degrees after their name! One disarmingly unpretentious man I exchanged cards with in London had "O.B.E." after his name indicating that he was an Officer of Order of the British Empire, a high honor bestowed for exceptional achievements. He was a joy to be with.

Once while working in Bogotá, Colombia, I went up to the rooftop restaurant of the lovely Hotel Tequendama to see the view and look at the menu. I thought I'd make a reservation for the following night, and I asked the maître d'hôtel for a table at 8 o'clock. He asked me in good but accented English if I liked to dance. Thinking he wanted to reserve a place for me at the show that followed dinner, I said yes. When he asked me if I'd care to go dancing with him I indignantly reminded him that he was the maître d'hôtel and that I had asked for a dinner reservation not a date. He apologized profusely, but laughed while explaining that he too was a guest at the hotel. He had just arrived from Mexico City, and was using the maître d'hôtel's phone to inquire about his lost luggage! Although I was embarrassed, I apologized and accepted his offer of dinner and dancing. Needless to say, I had a wonderful time.

Spend some time absorbing the culture of the locale. One of the best ways to learn to deal with your clients is to understand their background. Get a good map and walk around. It is interesting to observe the behavior patterns of the people. If you are fortunate enough to be working in a country that has a number of business and professional women in the workforce, you may want to see if they have organized into any associations or clubs. A visit with a group of working women will go far toward helping you understand the local business culture.

If you have the time, pretend you are a tourist and absorb the high points of the culture. Visit museums, galleries, shops and parks, or go to the theater or a concert. I once spent a day at the Museum of Anthropology in Mexico City and came away with a better understanding of the Mexican personality. On another trip, I spent a few hours in the Museum of Modern Art, also in Mexico City. I was amazed to find a superb exhibition of J.M.W. Turner, the nineteenth-century British painter. Noticing an attractive man, I remarked in Spanish about the light in Turner's works. He turned to me and replied in almost totally unaccented English that, on his recent business trip to New York, his colleagues had teased him about living in a cultural backwater. We exchanged cards and I wasn't a bit surprised to see that Federico Cabrera Rojas was a first vice president of Citibank de Mexico!

If you do meet a man and become emotionally involved with him, what will you do? Do not telex your company and tell them you're never coming back. Seriously, though, a long distance romance is difficult to sustain. Also, it's a good idea to get to know him better than the few days or weeks have allowed. Invite him to visit you the next time he's in the United States, or take your next vacation in his city, and then see how you feel. Most of the time the relationship will not work. But you didn't get this far in business by being either timid or foolish, so if you think it will work, do it!

In some places, such as mainland China, relationships between visitors and locals are discouraged. The Chinese themselves are not sure how close to foreigners they are allowed to get. Chinese businessmen often have to receive permission from their superiors before meeting foreign coworkers for lunch. There are occasionally penalties for those who fail to do so. As a foreigner your activities are limited mostly to business and sightseeing.

Of course, you will not be able to socialize with men in most of the Middle East. But, if you are so inclined, you can meet and date men in Israel, Egypt and even Jordan in much the same way as in Western societies.

Whether you are married or single, when you're homesick, you can meet people from the United States, no matter what country you're in. Most major cities have an American expatriate community where you might even find someone from your home town. Usually the U.S. Embassy will be able to give you information on contacting "expats," some of whom have been away for a while and would enjoy a visit from a businesswoman from the United States. Another way to meet Americans is to look up a group like the Brazilian-American or the British-American friendship club. You can find that type of association in many countries. These clubs often sponsor language classes, tours and social events that are usually of a high quality.

If all else fails and you're still homesick don't forget that McDonalds, Pizza Hut and Baskin Robbins can now be found around the globe. You can also eat in good American-style restaurants in Paris, London, Tokyo, Hong Kong and even Seoul, Korea. There is even a replica of Manhattan's Joe Allen Steak House in Paris. California nouvelle or Tex-Mex cooking, good burgers and New England clam chowder can be found in many cities. Don't forget that the American Clubs in Hong Kong, Beijing, Tokyo, Taipei and Singapore offer excellent food. Check if your own club has a reciprocal arrangement. Having a chili burger and a glass of California Zinfandel in Singapore may not be the same as being in the United States, but it's good to know you can have a little bit of home on the other side of the world.

11

Career, Love and Family: Having it All

It may be difficult to breastfeed your baby if you're 10,000 miles away on assignment in Jakarta, Indonesia, but that doesn't mean that you have to choose between your career and your family. One New York woman simply stated to her boss that for six months after the birth of her child she would not be able to travel farther than New Jersey. To her delight and surprise, he said, "Are you sure that's all the time you need? I was afraid you wouldn't travel for a year." Granted, not all bosses are that flexible, but don't underestimate your value to the corporation. A good number of employers may be willing to compromise about family situations rather than risk losing you. In fact, when one executive at a large corporation became pregnant, she was *promoted* to avoid the chance that she would quit.

So, you're in a fairly benevolent corporation, and you have options for advancement, overseas travel and family. Now, how do you go about having them all? In the past, women who rose high on the corporate ladder didn't have many options. The few executive women in the 1950s through the early 1970s often didn't marry or have children. They devoted themselves entirely to their careers. A recent poll of 300 executive women showed that 52 percent had either never married, were divorced or were widowed, and that 61 percent had no children.

Certainly, many of these women were programed in childhood to believe that being an executive was an unnatural condition for a woman. Today, any combination of roles and lifestyles is acceptable. Even if house-husbands are not exactly the norm, in the 1980s it is no longer the joke it once was.

Young executive women today are advancing further and faster than the women who proceeded them. In the past, most women were not on career tracks that involved travel, because travel was mostly the domain of those executives on the way up. Now, however, women are traveling domestically in record numbers, and traveling overseas with increased frequency. Another recent phenomenon is that male and female executives have begun traveling together. For a while there were complaints, reminiscent of the traditional policemen's wives' complaints about having female recruits in the patrol car. Today that cop's wife is often in the workforce, too—riding or traveling or strategizing with men. One woman executive said, "Nobody liked it in the beginning, but now men and women travel together. It's a non-event."

How can the married executive with children juggle her family, job and travel? In the best of all possible worlds, she should have a supportive, cooperative husband, a healthy well-adjusted child, responsible care for the child, an encouraging, understanding boss and an exciting job. Since this is rarely the case, serious long-term planning is required to manage this kind of juggling act. Most women go to college, and often graduate school, to prepare for a career. A four-year course of study isn't necessary to have a family, but *some* long-range planning should be part of a woman's preparation if she wants a husband, children and career.

Of course, you may want just a husband and career, or even just a career. Women today no longer need feel like outcasts for not wanting children or marriage. The "will-I-be-lonely-in-my-old-age" argument no longer carries much weight; patterns of aging and families have changed all that. I rarely see my 69-year-old widowed mother, even though she lives only 20 minutes away, because I'm constantly working and she's busy enjoying her recent retirement with her lover.

If you do marry a reasonable, caring man (and would you marry another kind?), discuss the choices and options available to you. If you are committed to having children, determine how your husband, boss and company can work with you to make things easier. The typical corporate child-care policy is light years away from being comprehensive, but these policies aren't standardized, so find out what is available to you. Some corporations provide child-care facilities, flextime and/or special financial and other allowance for child-care, or will assist you in finding a suitable housekeeper. Since over 60 percent of all U.S. families (at all levels) are two-career couples, and over 53 percent of women with children work outside the home, it is time for child-care to become a part of every company's benefit structure. See what you can negotiate with your employer—you may be pleasantly surprised.

Women today also have the option of postponing having children until their late 30s if they wish. Many fast-trackers build their reputation over 10 or 12 years and then take some time out for childbearing, often without losing ground in their careers.

If you decide to have a child try to plan your next full year to your best advantage. Of course, you can travel during most of your pregnancy, although you probably won't want to during the last three months. Study your job and plan your schedule as best you can to accommodate both child and career.

While hardly a universal trend, younger men seem to be more willing to share home and family responsibilities. Those men who were weaned on Betty Friedan show more initiative in taking care of children, cooking and nurturing. The majority of men over 40, on the other hand, find it hard to escape the bonds of their traditional upbringing, except for the older men whose consciousness has been raised by their liberated daughters. Men born or raised since the start of the women's movement, appear to be more sensitive and flexible than older men.

Most men are willing at least to lend a hand with the housework. If you make a lot of money, arguments over who does what can be avoided by employing a housekeeper. Otherwise it might be a good idea to discuss dividing up the chores in some fashion. Of course, if you are on the road for a stretch of time, it's somewhat difficult to clean the house or prepare meals. Just as in your international deals, negotiation is always better than confrontation. Involve your husband or partner in finding ways to manage time more effectively.

Things are somewhat easier if you're married or living with someone and *don't* have children. In this case you only have adult sensibilities to be concerned with. There is no question that your time away from home can strain your relationship. What you must do is see your overseas travel as a means to an end—it may help your career take off, or give you the increased earnings to buy a home, or it may give you options for a different kind of career in the future. Eventually, you may be happier getting off the fast track and devoting more time to home, hobbies or friends. But right now your overseas experience is increasing your options for the future.

What if your husband or partner resents your time away? (You may resent it yourself sometimes.) Here again, you must help him see how your travel will improve your future together. Ask him to help you improve the time you do spend together. Explain that sometimes it's good for couples to be separated for a short time and that separation can refresh a relationship. My husband uses the time that I'm away to catch up on horror movies, neglect the household chores, eat Chinese food out of cartons and go to jazz concerts. Most of these are things that I don't enjoy so we rarely do them together. For both of us it's healthy to occasionally not have to relate to and please each other. And the homecomings are exhilarating and exciting.

Most solid relationships don't break up because one partner is on the road from time to time. But if your relationship is shaky to begin with, traveling can put more strain on it. Success can also strain an already troubled relationship, especially if you make more money than your partner. Some men are unhappy in relationships where they feel like the less powerful person. Many of them grew up never even knowing a professional woman, much less one who travels internationally and makes a high salary. Talking about it is the best way to overcome differences.

On the other hand, many men like, or at least don't resent, the fact that their wife travels and earns a lot of money. These men are able to enjoy the perks of your career (not the least of which is a second income). Some companies will give you a day or two in compensatory time if you've been away for a while. Or you can take a few days off before or after your travel to spend with your husband. If this is not possible, ask him to meet you in London for a long weekend when you're working there, or see if he can take his vacation and accompany you to Rio de Janeiro. My husband thoroughly enjoyed seeing me off to work in Rio each morning while he had a leisurely breakfast on the hotel terrace. He spent his time swimming, sightseeing and drinking piña coladas while I spent the day in meetings. Then we would have dinner together and spend an hour in one of Rio's beautiful nightspots. He feels good that all the responsibilities are not the sole province of men anymore. He, like many other men today, is secure enough to enjoy the benefits of female careerism.

Another difficult situation is that of the single woman. If you are traveling fairly often, it's not easy to get momentum into a relationship. Relationships need care and nurturing at all times, but the beginning is the most delicate period. If your boyfriend overreacts to your traveling, tell him that you will be thinking of when you return during all of your waking moments. If either of you use the short separations as reason for avoiding the relationship then you are probably not right for each other anyway.

If you're away regularly you may find it difficult even to meet a man. See if you can schedule a fairly long period where you don't travel overseas. August is a good time, as Europe and many other countries are all on vacation. Try to take your vacation in a resort near your home town, or go to museums and play tourist at home. Answer or place a personal ad in a reputable publication, or take flying, ballooning, language or rafting lessons if that's what you've always wanted to do. All of the above are fun and will definitely put you in the company of quite a few men.

Women with husbands and children and single women must both adjust to the changes of separation, but the pressures on the single mother may be the most intense. If you are committed to your child and to a job that takes you away from home, quality child-care is essential. If you have a parent who is healthy and willing to care for your child while you're away, don't hesitate to ask for help. You may not be sure your parents brought you up in the best way possible but at least the child will be with your family. If parents or other relatives are unable to keep your child during your trip, make sure you find the best care available. Start looking far in advance of the trip. It's important that the child (and you) get to know and trust the caretaker. Also, prepare the child for your trip. Explain where you're going and why. Take out maps and globes and show the child where you're going. Tell the child about the new bike or computer the money you are earning will buy. Most of all, reassure the child that you will return, and give the date. If you are delayed, call the child and explain. If the child is too young to understand, tell him or her anyway. Saying you love the child and that you'll only be in Cairo for two weeks will make *you* feel better about the separation.

Another good idea is to tape record messages for your children before you leave so they will be able to hear your voice whenever they want to. If you're away for an extended period of time you can also express mail a tape to them. Ask your husband or friends to tape the children, too, and have the tapes sent to you. Calls at regular intervals are important for you and your family. If things are going moderately well at home, you will feel much better after a call.

A Note on Relocation: With the focus of business becoming broader and more global, many women today are considering the possibility of relocating, whether to another city in the United States or overseas. While relocating in the United States may be an inconvenience, the problems surrounding becoming an expatriate executive can be enormous. However, so are the rewards. For a single woman with no strong family ties, a stint overseas offers tremendous opportunity with little risk. For a married person with or without children, there is much more to consider before making the decision to relocate overseas.

Some of the problems begin to show up when a female manager is in line for an overseas assignment. Many corporations believe that while women are qualified to manage effectively overseas, they will not be accepted as well as men. This is pretty much the same argument used by the senior management (usually male) in resisting women's efforts to travel overseas for short-term business. If you feel that a long-term overseas assignment will benefit your career, make your feelings known.

On the other hand, you must also try to determine what long-term plans your company has for you. Although the practice is infrequent, some companies have sent men and women to undesirable posts to get them off the fast track.

If you're offered an overseas assignment, first consider the length of the stay. A six-month assignment is a lot different from a two-to-three-year assignment, and involves far less dislocation for you and yours. In a long-term assignment, you may have to sell your house or give up or sublet your rental apartment, say goodbye to friends, parents and all that is familiar and prepare to immerse yourself in a very different culture and live by its value system. Essentially you must begin life over. Married women must also take their husbands' career and children's schooling into account.

For many people, the change is exhilarating and a definite growth experience. One banker who was disheartened at how New York was constantly becoming dirtier, more dangerous and more expensive, competitive and unfriendly was thrilled to get an offer to relocate herself and her family to Hong Kong. Her husband, an insurance company executive, was able to transfer to a subsidiary of his company in Hong Kong. Since their children were young, three and five years old, it was a relatively easy and agreeable transition for all.

One of the most important factors in relocation is where you're being sent. Adjustment to Western Europe, particularly the major capitals, is fairly easy. However, an assignment to Bangkok is another thing. For some people, the cultural differences may be too much to handle.

If a married couple's relationship is a good one, the stresses of relocation can often be overcome. But don't expect the excitement of a new place to improve a failing marriage. Things can only get worse in a strange country, especially if your husband has trouble finding work. In some countries, he may be breaking the law merely by looking for a job in competition with local workers.

If a position in another country opens up, find out first about the country, and then about your proposed job in it and what is planned for you when you return to the United States. Your next step is to discuss the move with your family and friends. If, on balance, the position you are in line for in

Tegucigalpa, Honduras is so full of problems for your personal and social life, it may not be worth the anticipated promotion two years later. One woman in such a situation felt that her company was forcing her out with an implied "transfer or leave" attitude. She did leave, but to another company and a better position.

If you have examined all the considerations, and you still feel that relocation is right for you, there are many ways to benefit from the situation. You will undoubtedly become fluent in a foreign language, learn international business practices and even be able to travel extensively in the region. You will gain sophistication and a perspective of the world that few people ever have the opportunity to acquire. A stint in a foreign country can be one of the most enriching times of your life.

You will have the most satisfaction from an overseas post if you are energetic, flexible, strongly motivated, have strong interpersonal skills and a sense of humor. It's easiest to adjust if you are married and your husband is able to work in the country, you are childless or have either very young or grown children and you are excited by and interested in the country. But not all of these factors are prerequisite for success. Even if your husband can't work at his regular job while overseas, he may be able to take a leave of absence from his company and spend the year abroad teaching English or writing the novel he has never had time for. Your relocation may turn out to be the opportunity he has been hoping for.

If you do go, make sure you are going for the right reasons. Wanting to get away from a bad personal or professional situation is usually a poor reason to relocate.

Making sure you are compatible with the culture is almost as important as the nature of your assignment. In fact, they are two sides of the same coin. Don't take an attractive assignment thinking you'll adjust to what you initially feel is an alien culture. You won't. A dynamic single lawyer friend of mine was offered a post in Mexico City. Although she was a third-generation Hispanic American, she welcomed the opportunity to get closer to her "roots." Needless to say, she is thriving, both professionally and personally. On the other hand, a banker acquaintance and "Japanophile" who was hoping for a post in Japan was offered a post in Singapore. She accepted it thinking she would learn to like it as much as Japan. She couldn't adjust to Singapore, and had to return to the United States before her assignment was completed.

Having to return home before your tour is up can be more detrimental to your career than declining the post in the first place. Discuss the assignment with management and find out in what ways the company is prepared to assist your transition from the United States. Some questions you can ask include: Does the company provide language and culture training for you, your husband and children? Will the company assist your husband in obtaining a work permit if he needs it? Could your husband transfer to your company if his skills match, and could he be assigned overseas as well? What assistance does the company give in finding and paying for housing, household help, schools, accounting, legal and tax advice, medical care, cars and pre- and post-assignment counseling?

Equally important are the questions regarding the job. How often you will be communicating with the home office and to whom in the office you will be reporting will give you an indication of your position in the hierarchy while overseas. If you see the post as a possible dumping ground, this is the time to find out, not when you are already overseas. Ask for a written guarantee of a job similar to or at a step up from the one you are leaving. The answers you get will tell you what the company plans for your career with them.

You may, if you accept a foreign position, find yourself living at a higher standard than in the United States. Servants are very inexpensive in the developing world and most middle-class people have at least one or two. The perks of cars, club membership and general entree into upper-class status may be hard to let go of when you return home.

If you are single and find that you have fallen in love with the handsome young local who has been pursuing you for a year, you may find him hard to let go of as well. In any case, you could always request another tour of duty from your company. Failing that, and depending on your feelings for the place, you could stay and work for a local company.

The great majority of expatriate executives go home enriched but anxious about the changes they will find. Don't worry, you'll be able to adjust to them and keep right on going up the corporate ladder.

12

Women in the World Marketplace: 2000 A.D.

In a 1978 perfume commercial a woman sings to her husband about her superwoman abilities. In the revised 1984 version of the commercial, she still claims superwoman status, but asks her husband for a little help occasionally. At this rate of change the commercial may have to be scrapped completely in five years. By then, hopefully, superwoman will no longer have to prove herself or ask for help from her husband. He will participate more equally in the housekeeping and child-rearing tasks without having to be asked. If the present trends continue, men will be assuming their share of the tasks with genuine interest and enthusiasm. While on the surface, women will gain the most, in fact, men will also benefit in ways that their fathers never dreamed of.

This change is already beginning. Most men today would not be happy to come home to a woman who has spent the day at home as their mothers often did. They seek out women who have stimulating lives. Most of these men today reject the idea of a relationship with a woman who lives vicariously through her husband. The responsibility of being the strong silent breadwinner has been overwhelming to most men.

In the future, we will see a blurring of traditional male/female roles. Most importantly, though, men and women will have *options*. While many men will continue to function in a fairly traditional fashion, they will also have the opportunity to pursue less traditional lifestyles if they wish. There is already growing acceptance for men who stay home with children full or part-time. Men can be, and often are, as nurturing as women. It is only their past conditioning that makes some men unemotional.

We are beginning to see new flexibility in love and work relationships. Men and women are taking turns caring for children. It is also no longer unusual for a female attorney to be married to a brilliant, struggling musician, or for a corporate vice president, also female, to be married to a graduate student of anthropology. Nor will it be unheard of for a man to take a break from a career that is no longer satisfying to pursue other options.

In this new equality, everybody wins. I have spoken to a number of young men who are delighted that they are married to or living with high-power, high-salaried women. They expressed a sense of relief at not having to assume the financial and emotional burdens alone. Some men expressed embarrassed pleasure at being able to pursue "feminine" tasks such as child nurturing, cooking, shopping and so on. Children are winners, too. Men spend more time with children when women work. Children identify more positively with mothers who work. However, in a 1984 *New York Times* magazine article, the three-year old daughter of a then superwoman said she wanted to be a father when she grew up, "because mommies work too hard." For most children whose mothers have relatively satisfying careers, a healthy attitude is conveyed to them about combining work and family.

Women will continue to have more options than ever, both at home and in the workplace. Telecommuting for example is a great boon for mothers (and fathers) of very young children. While the climb up the corporate ladder hasn't been as fast as most women would like, it is only for the last 10 or 15 years at most that substantial numbers of women have been at managerial levels and above. It will probably take at least another 10–15 years before large numbers of women will be at the highest levels of the corporate hierarchy. But already, executive women are being sought to fill outside directorships on corporate boards in large numbers.

Change is coming in all sectors of the workforce. It is commonplace to see road signs saying "People Working" instead of "Men Working" at construction sites throughout the United States. Many traditional male preserves are seeing women in their ranks.

Women poured into business and professional schools in the 1970s, able at last to compete in the careers that were for so long closed to them. While many women are making tremendous inroads in law, business, engineering and economics, others are dissatisfied with the rate of progress or feel poorly compensated for ten-hour workdays and seven-day workweeks. A fair number of women are leaving those jobs to write, consult and open their own businesses. One of the most significant changes today is the increase of women-owned businesses. Of the approximately 12,000 new businesses started each week, almost one third are owned by women. These entrepreneurs are involved in every type of venture: manufacturing, architecture, accounting, real estate, as well as the traditional women-owned businesses. There are major organizations on the national and local levels, such as National Association of Women Business Owners, the National Alliance of Home-Based Businesswomen (with men as 10 percent of its membership) and the Women Business Owners of New York, whose memberships are skyrocketing. From 1977 to 1980 alone there was a 33 percent increase in women-owned businesses! During the same period the number of women-owned construction companies rose almost 25 percent. That's progress!

Since the United States is often the international catalyst for change, we can hope that some of the progress women have made will set an example for change overseas. Gains have been coming elsewhere in the developed world, although slowly. While women have owned small businesses and been in the professions for a long time in the Common Market countries, they have not made much progress yet in the corporate marketplace, even though they make up 40 percent of the workforce. Two large European banks have recently opened "women's branches" to serve workingwomen in Geneva and Edinburgh. The International Federation of Business and Professional Women has more than 250,000 members.

In the developing world, progress is even slower. Women make up 60 to 80 percent of the agricultural workers in Africa and Asia and more than 40 percent of those in Latin America. Even here, through their own efforts and those of U.S. businesswomen's associations, many of these women are organizing into cooperatives and communes. They are learning that economic power is personal power.

Some women in the developing world are small business owners. They are becoming part of a system that will free them from the extreme poverty of many in their countries. This progress is sure to continue. It is my greatest wish to revise this book in the coming years to read "When in Brazil (Great Britain, Taiwan, Honduras, Ghana, Italy . . .) be sure to ask your client for *her* recommendations."

Bibliography

Adler, N. "Expecting International Success: Female Managers Overseas." *Columbia Journal of World Business*. Fall 1984.

_____. "Women in International Management: Where Are They?" *California Management Review*, Summer 1984.

Cateora, P. *International Marketing*, 5th ed. Richard Irwin Inc. 1983.

Condon, J. "Foreign Female Executives: Japan's 'Third Gender.' " *Wall Street Journal*, April 2, 1984.

Hill, J.S. and Still, R.R. "Adapting Products to LDC Tastes." *Harvard Business Review*, March–April 1984.

Lanier, A. "Your Manager Abroad: How Welcome, How Prepared?" *AMACOM* (American Management Association), 1975.

Rossman, M.L. "Japanese Foreign Market Entry Strategies in Latin America." *Baylor Business Studies*, August–October 1982.

_____. "The Five Nations of Latin America." *Marketing News* (American Marketing Association), October 11, 1985.

Seligman, S.D. "A Shirtsleeves Guide to Corporate Chinese Etiquette." *The China Business Review*, January–February 1983.

Van Zandt, H. "How to Negotiate in Japan." *Harvard Business Review*, November–December 1970.

About the Author

Marlene L. Rossman is a consultant, author and professor who specializes in marketing and international business. Her firm, Rossman, Graham Associates in New York City, does marketing consulting for U.S. and foreign businesses. Ms. Rossman teaches international marketing at the Graduate School of Business of Iona College and marketing at New York University, where she also leads seminars for women executives on doing business overseas. She has written and lectured on marketing strategies, international trade and women in business.

Ms. Rossman was born in New York City, where she received a B.A. in English from Pace University, an M.A. in Linguistics from New York University and an M.B.A. in Marketing and International Business from Pace University. She lives in Manhattan with her husband, Elliot Silverman, a lawyer.